READING *the* BIBLE *through* LENT

READING *the* BIBLE *through* LENT

All the daily Lenten scripture readings from the Catholic liturgy, with guidance for Lectio Divina

Commentaries by ADRIAN GRAFFY

DARTON·LONGMAN+TODD

This book is dedicated to
Carlos Castillo Mattasoglio

First published in Great Britain in 2023 by
Darton, Longman and Todd Ltd
1 Spencer Court
140 – 142 Wandsworth High Street
London
SW18 4JJ

© 2023 Adrian Graffy

ISBN: 978-1-915412-08-9

The right of Adrian Graffy to be identified as the Author of this work has been asserted in accordance with the Copyright, Designs and Patents Act 1988.

Bible extracts taken from The Revised New Jerusalem Bible, published and copyright © 2019 by Darton, Longman and Todd and The Crown Publishing Group, a division of Penguin Random House LLC, New York.

A catalogue record for this book is available from the British Library.

Designed and produced by Judy Linard
Olive tree illustration © Artur Balitskii/Dreamstime.com
Printed and bound in Great Britain by Short Run Press Ltd, Exeter

CONTENTS

INTRODUCTION   7

THE FIRST DAYS OF LENT   9
Ash Wednesday (three readings)   11
Thursday after Ash Wednesday   14
Friday after Ash Wednesday   15
Saturday after Ash Wednesday   18

FIRST WEEK IN LENT   21
First Sunday of Lent: Year A (three readings)   23
First Sunday of Lent: Year B (three readings)   26
First Sunday of Lent: Year C (three readings)   28
Monday   31
Tuesday   34
Wednesday   35
Thursday   37
Friday   39
Saturday   41

SECOND WEEK IN LENT   45
Second Sunday of Lent: Year A (three readings)   47
Second Sunday of Lent: Year B (three readings)   49
Second Sunday of Lent: Year C (three readings)   52
Monday   55
Tuesday   56
Wednesday   58
Thursday   60
Friday   63
Saturday   65

THIRD WEEK IN LENT   69
Third Sunday of Lent: Year A (three readings)   71
Third Sunday of Lent: Year B (three readings)   75

READING THE BIBLE THROUGH LENT

Third Sunday of Lent: Year C (three readings)	78
Monday	81
Tuesday	83
Wednesday	86
Thursday	88
Friday	90
Saturday	92

FOURTH WEEK IN LENT — 95

Fourth Sunday of Lent: Year A (three readings)	97
Fourth Sunday of Lent: Year B (three readings)	101
Fourth Sunday of Lent: Year C (three readings)	104
Monday	107
Tuesday	109
Wednesday	111
Thursday	114
Friday	117
Saturday	119

FIFTH WEEK IN LENT — 121

Fifth Sunday of Lent: Year A (three readings)	123
Fifth Sunday of Lent: Year B (three readings)	126
Fifth Sunday of Lent: Year C (three readings)	129
Monday	132
Tuesday	136
Wednesday	139
Thursday	141
Friday	143
Saturday	146

HOLY WEEK — 149

Palm Sunday of the Passion of the Lord: Year A (three readings)	151
Palm Sunday of the Passion of the Lord: Year B (three readings)	159
Palm Sunday of the Passion of the Lord: Year C (three readings)	165
Monday	171
Tuesday	173
Wednesday	176
Holy Thursday: Chrism Mass (three readings)	178
Holy Thursday: Evening Mass of the Lord's Supper (three readings)	180
Good Friday (three readings)	183

INTRODUCTION

THE CHRISTIAN JOURNEY THROUGH the season of Lent is assisted by the word of God. The lectionary provides a rich programme of readings from the books of the Old and New Testaments, from the Scriptures of the Jewish faith and those of Christianity.

Lent is a preparation for the celebration of the paschal mystery of Christ's death and resurrection. Some are preparing in Lent for Christian baptism and rebirth in Jesus Christ. Others look forward to the annual solemn renewal of baptismal commitments.

The readings on the first days of Lent focus on Christian renewal initially through prayer, fasting and almsgiving, and encourage the strong Christian virtues of forgiveness, perseverance, solidarity and steadfastness in suffering.

The responsorial psalms after the first reading, which are related to the readings, often suggest avenues of preaching, prayer and meditation.

The Lenten gospels are chosen initially from the synoptic gospels, and from week four onwards from the fourth gospel. The gospels of the Sunday lectionary take us from the synoptic accounts of the temptation of Christ and his transfiguration, on the first two Sundays, to the Johannine 'signs' of living water, light and life on the subsequent Sundays in Year A. These magnificent gospel passages, from John chapters 4, 9 and 11, can be chosen every year if considered helpful, since they highlight the journey in faith which reaches its climax at Easter.

The Holy Week readings of the Passion gospels invite the participation of all those present, with the synoptic narratives read in sequence on Palm Sunday, and the Johannine presentation reserved for Good Friday. The Songs of the suffering servant from the second part of Isaiah accompany and illuminate the gospels of Holy Week, as we draw ever closer to the celebration of the mystery of the death and resurrection at the paschal Triduum.

The commentaries provided here consider all the Lenten readings from Ash Wednesday to Good Friday inclusive and are designed to support the preacher, the reader and the listener. Each gospel reading is followed by a question and a suggestion for prayer. The full text of the Scripture readings is given from the *Revised New Jerusalem Bible*, edited by Dom Henry Wansbrough, and published by Darton, Longman and Todd in 2019. It is a vibrant new translation, building on the noble Jerusalem Bible tradition, and enriched by the latest biblical scholarship.

Fr Adrian Graffy, Scripture scholar and member of the Pontifical Biblical Commission since 2014, provides the commentaries. His *Sunday Gospels for Advent, Christmas, Lent and Easter* and *Sunday Gospels for Ordinary Time* were published by Darton, Longman and Todd in 2020 and 2021.

The First Days of Lent

ASH WEDNESDAY

A reading from the prophet Joel (2:12-18)
'So now – declares the LORD -
come back to me with all your heart,
fasting, weeping, mourning.'
Tear your hearts and not your clothes
and come back to the LORD your God,
for he is gracious and compassionate,
slow to anger, rich in faithful love,
and he relents from inflicting disaster.
Who knows if he will not return,
relent and leave a blessing behind him,
a grain offering and a libation
for the LORD your God?

Blow the ram's-horn in Zion!
Order a fast, proclaim a solemn assembly,
call the people together,
summon the community,
assemble the elders, gather the children,
even infants at the breast!
Call the bridegroom from his bedroom
and the bride from her canopy!
Between portico and altar let the priests,
the ministers of the LORD, weep,
saying, 'Spare your people, LORD!
Do not expose your heritage to contempt,
to the sarcasm of the nations!
Why should it be said among the peoples,
"Where is their God?"'
Then, becoming jealous over his land,
the LORD took pity on his people.

READING THE BIBLE THROUGH LENT

COMING BACK, RETURNING, to God is the challenge of Lent. This is not an external journey, but something of the heart. The prophet Joel, in the time after the exile to Babylon, describes the God who awaits our return with words given to Moses in Exodus 34:6. God is rich in 'faithful love', *hesed*, and 'slow to anger'. After the devastation of a plague of locusts (Joel 2:3-5), God will restore the blessings of grain and wine. The urgent call to repent has the people react quickly: even the bride and groom leave their wedding chamber. God is portrayed as 'jealous over his land', protective of people, and quick to 'take pity'.

> **Psalm 51 (50)** The *Miserere* is a penitential psalm traditionally attributed to David, who pleads for forgiveness for his great sins (2 Samuel 11), but later verses – 'rebuild Jerusalem' – show the psalm to be of much later date. Fervent joy is the gift of the Lord, who opens our mouths in praise.

A reading from the second letter of St Paul to the Corinthians (5:20 – 6:2)

Therefore we are ambassadors for Christ, since God is appealing through us: on Christ's behalf we beg you, be reconciled to God. He who knew no sin he made sin for our sake, so that in him we might become the righteousness of God.

As fellow-workers we appeal to you also not to accept the grace of God in vain, for he says: *At an acceptable time I listened to you, and in the day of salvation I helped you.* See, now is the acceptable time; see, now is the day of salvation.

PAUL AND HIS FELLOW-WORKERS are ambassadors speaking for Christ, delivering God's appeal for 'reconciliation'. This is only possible because God made Christ into sin 'for our sake', immersing him in humanity, with all its faults, so that we might become in him God's 'justness', God's 'righteousness'. We are invited not to waste the grace of God, which comes at the 'right time', the *kairos,* and on the 'day of salvation'. With the repetition of the Greek word *nun* Paul stresses that the words of Scripture (Isaiah 49:8) are fulfilled 'now'.

THE FIRST DAYS OF LENT

A reading from the holy gospel according to Matthew (6:1-6, 16-18)

Jesus said to his disciples: 'Be careful not to parade your righteousness before others to be seen by them; otherwise you will have no reward from your Father in heaven. So whenever you give alms, do not sound a trumpet before you as hypocrites do in the synagogues and in the streets to win human admiration. Amen I say to you, they have had their reward. But when you give alms, your left hand must not know what your right is doing, so that your almsgiving may be in secret, and your Father who sees all that is done in secret will reward you.

'And whenever you pray, do not be like hypocrites: they love to pray standing in the synagogues and at street corners for people to see them. Amen I say to you, they have had their reward. But whenever you pray, go to your private room, shut yourself in, and pray to your Father who is in that secret place, and your Father who sees in secret will reward you.

'Whenever you fast, do not put on a gloomy look as hypocrites do: they go about looking unsightly to show others they are fasting. Amen I say to you, they have had their reward. But when you fast, put oil on your head and wash your face, so that you may not seem to others to be fasting but only to your Father in secret; and your Father who sees in secret will reward you.'

IN THIS PASSAGE FROM the Sermon on the Mount Jesus warns the disciples not to 'parade' their righteousness (*dikaiosyne*). If you make a spectacle of your good deeds, this will be your reward. A trio of teaching considers almsgiving, prayer and fasting, with thrice repeated phrases: do not be 'hypocrites'; 'Amen I say to you they have had their reward'; 'do things in secret' where 'your Father sees'. The hypocrite wears a mask of righteousness while his heart is far away; he prefers the praise of the world, but true righteousness is done in secret. The words about oil on the head and a washed face are an unsettling challenge to public forms of penance.

Have I experienced the faithful love and pity of God?
For those who parade their piety, we pray to the Lord.

READING THE BIBLE THROUGH LENT

THURSDAY AFTER ASH WEDNESDAY

A reading from the book of Deuteronomy (30:15-20)

Moses said to the people: 'Look, today I am offering you life and prosperity, death and disaster. If you obey the commandments of the Lord your God, which I am laying down for you today, if you love the Lord your God and follow his ways, if you keep his commandments, his laws and his customs, you will live and grow numerous, and the Lord your God will bless you in the land which you are entering and make your own. But if your heart turns away, if you refuse to listen, if you let yourself be drawn into worshipping other gods and serving them, I tell you today, you will most certainly perish; you will not live for long in the land which you are crossing the Jordan to enter and possess. Today, I call heaven and earth to witness against you: I am offering you life or death, blessing or curse. Choose life, then, so that you and your descendants may live, in the love of the Lord your God, obeying his voice, holding fast to him; for in this your life consists, and on this depends the length of time that you stay in the land which the Lord swore to your ancestors Abraham, Isaac and Jacob that he would give them.'

THE FINAL BOOK OF the Pentateuch, Deuteronomy, comprises several speeches of Moses. The reading today is taken from the last great speech, before the account of Moses' ascent of Mount Nebo and his death (Deuteronomy 34). To live as a human being is to choose: our choices have consequences. To turn away from God, to serve false gods, leads to disaster. To choose to obey God's law of life is to rely on the trustworthy God who has already spoken to the ancestors, and who will protect us in the present and in the future.

> **Psalm 1** The theme of choice continues. The first psalm expresses a blessing on those who delight in the law of the Lord, who are compared to a tree standing strong beside flowing waters. Not so are the wicked, who are like 'winnowed chaff', at the mercy of the wind.

THE FIRST DAYS OF LENT

A reading from the holy gospel according to Luke (9:22-25)

Jesus said to his disciples: 'The Son of man must suffer much, and be rejected by the elders and chief priests and scribes and be put to death, and on the third day be raised up.'

Then, speaking to all, he said, 'Anyone who wants to be a follower of mine, must renounce self and take up the cross every day and follow me. For whoever wants to save life will lose it; but whoever loses life for my sake, will save it. What does it profit someone to gain the whole world while losing or forfeiting self?'

FOLLOWING PETER'S CONFESSION that Jesus is 'Messiah', Jesus speaks to the disciples for the first time about the suffering and death he foresees. Jesus knows what awaits him in Jerusalem. At the same time, he announces that he will be 'raised up on the third day'. The choice put before Israel, to 'choose life', is starkly redrawn here as Jesus invites everyone to take up 'the cross', and be ready to 'lose life'. The willingness to lose life is in fact an option for life. The journey of Jesus to Jerusalem, which is about to begin, will demonstrate this truth.

Recall the sacrifices you have made, and see how they led to life.
For those who cling, that the Lord will grant them freedom.

FRIDAY AFTER ASH WEDNESDAY

A reading from the prophet Isaiah (58:1-9)

Thus says the Lord:
'Shout for all you are worth, do not hold back;
raise your voice like a trumpet.
Proclaim to my people their rebellions,
to the House of Jacob, their sins.
They seek me day after day,
they delight to know my ways,
like a nation that has acted righteously
and not forsaken the law of its God.

They ask me for righteous judgements;
to be near God is their delight.
"Why should we fast, if you do not see,
why humble ourselves if you never notice?"
Look, you seek your own pleasure on your fastdays
and you exploit all your workmen;
look, you fast only to quarrel and squabble
and strike viciously with your fist.
Fasting like yours today
will never make your voice heard on high.
Is that the sort of fast that pleases me,
a day of self-humiliation?
Hanging your head like a reed,
making a bed of sackcloth and ashes?
Is that what you call fasting,
a day acceptable to the LORD?
Is not this the sort of fast that I favour:
to open unjust fetters,
to undo the straps of the yoke,
to let the oppressed go free
and to break every yoke?
Is it not sharing your food with the hungry,
bringing into your house the homeless poor,
clothing one you see to lack clothing,
not drawing back from your own kin?
Then your light will blaze out like the dawn
and your wound will quickly be healed.
Saving justice will go ahead of you
and the glory of the LORD come behind you.
Then you will call to the LORD and he will answer;
you will cry and he will say, "I am here."'

ISAIAH CHAPTER 58 IS shared between the first readings today and tomorrow. Through the voice of this post-exilic prophet God speaks at length about fasting. Selfish behaviour and exploitation of others make fasting useless. Fasting is not to be a pretence: 'hanging your head like a reed', and 'making a bed of sackcloth and ashes'. The true priorities of the religious person are to 'open unjust fetters', 'to undo the straps of the yoke', to 'share your food with the hungry' and 'to bring into your house the homeless poor'. These ancient words have an immediate impact for today. The person who behaves like this will be light for others, and experience rapid healing. Justice will precede them, and the glory of the Lord will follow them. Their calls to the Lord will be answered.

> **Psalm 51 (50)** The psalmist, in further verses from the *Miserere*, acknowledges guilt and offers in sacrifice a contrite spirit and a humbled heart.

A reading from the holy gospel according to Matthew (9:14-15)

Then John's disciples came to him and said, 'Why do we and the Pharisees fast, but your disciples do not?' Jesus replied, 'Surely the bridegroom's attendants cannot mourn as long as the bridegroom is still with them? But the days will come when the bridegroom is taken away from them, and then they will fast.'

ENCOUNTER WITH OTHER RELIGIOUS groups will be a feature of Jesus' ministry. The behaviour of Jesus and his disciples causes consternation among the followers of John and of the Pharisees, since they do not fast. Jesus assumes the role of the bridegroom, reminding us of God's marriage covenant with Israel. The wedding feast, at which his disciples are guests, will indeed be interrupted, when the 'bridegroom will be taken away' and handed over for death. The wedding-supper of Jesus the Lamb will be restored at the end of time (Apocalypse 19).

How does the presence of Jesus change everything?
For people who will not allow Jesus to change them, let us pray.

SATURDAY AFTER ASH WEDNESDAY

A reading from the prophet Isaiah (58:9-14)

The Lord says this:
'If you banish the yoke from among you,
the pointed finger and malicious gossip,
if you share what you have with the hungry
and satisfy the needs of the deprived,
your light will rise in the darkness
and your darkest hour will be like noon.
The LORD will always guide you,
will satisfy your needs in arid land;
he will give strength to your bones
and you will be like a watered garden,
like a flowing spring whose waters never run dry.
Your ancient ruins will be rebuilt;
age-old foundations will rise up.
You will be called "Breach-mender", "Restorer-of-streets-to-live-in".
If you refrain from trampling the Sabbath,
from taking your own pleasure on my holy day,
if you call the Sabbath "a delight"
and the day sacred to the LORD "a day honoured",
if you honour it by not going your own way,
from seeking your own pleasure and idle chatter,
then you will find true pleasure in the LORD
and I shall let you ride over the heights of the land.
I shall feed you on the heritage of your father Jacob,
for the mouth of the LORD has spoken.'

THE PROPHET CONTINUES TO deliver words of the Lord about fasting. Banishing 'the yoke' and providing for those in need are the real priority, not adherence to human rules. When such new behaviour is established, the prophet repeats, 'your light will rise in the darkness, and your darkness will be like noon'. The imagery is now strong and positive: 'a watered garden', 'a flowing spring', 'rebuilt ruins'. Honouring the Sabbath will bring 'true pleasure in the Lord'. In a chariot or on a camel (Isaiah 60:6) 'I shall let you ride over the heights of the land'. The promises made of old are fulfilled.

THE FIRST DAYS OF LENT

> **Psalm 86 (85)** The psalmist describes himself as 'the servant who trusts in you', and prays, 'give joy to the soul of your servant, Lord, for to you I lift up my soul.'

A reading from the holy gospel according to Luke (5:27-32)

After this he went out and noticed a tax collector, Levi by name, sitting at the tax office, and said to him, 'Follow me.' And leaving everything he got up and followed him.

And Levi held a great reception for Jesus in his house, and with them at table was a large crowd of tax collectors and others. The Pharisees and their scribes kept complaining to his disciples saying, 'Why do you eat and drink with tax collectors and sinners?' Jesus said to them in reply, 'It is not the healthy who need a doctor, but the sick. I have come to call not the righteous but sinners to conversion.'

IN INVITING LEVI TO be a disciple Jesus is breaking new ground, for tax collectors were considered to be dishonest and disloyal. Yet Levi is just as willing to leave everything as are those who left their fishing boats. The banquet for Levi's colleagues 'and others' shows the universality of the invitation Jesus offers, preparing places particularly for the sick and the sinful.

Is our outreach as warm and generous as that of Jesus?
For those who hesitate at the threshold, uncertain of being welcomed, let us pray.

First Week in Lent

FIRST SUNDAY OF LENT – YEAR A

A reading from the book of Genesis (2:7-9, 3:1-7)

The Lord God shaped man from the dust of the ground and breathed the breath of life into his nostrils, and man became a living being. The Lord God planted a garden in Eden in the east, and there put the man he had shaped. From the soil, the Lord God caused to grow every kind of tree, pleasant to look at and good to eat, with the tree of life in the middle of the garden, and the tree of the knowledge of good and evil.

Now, the snake was the most cunning of all the wild animals that the Lord God had made. It asked the woman, 'Did God really say you were not to eat from any of the trees in the garden?' The woman answered the snake, 'We may eat the fruit of the trees in the garden. It was of the fruit of the tree in the middle of the garden that God said, "You must not eat it, nor touch it, under pain of death."' Then the snake said to the woman, 'No! You will not die! God knows that the day you eat it your eyes will be opened and you will be like gods, knowing good from evil.' The woman saw that the tree was good to eat and pleasing to the eye, and that it was desirable for the wisdom that it could give. So she took some of its fruit and ate it. She also gave some to her husband who was with her, and he ate it. Then the eyes of both of them were opened and they realised that they were naked. So they sewed fig leaves together to make themselves loincloths.

IT IS NO SURPRISE that the first reading on the first Sunday of Lent takes us back to the beginnings. This story of the creation of human beings, from the earth and the breath of God, reminds us of a profound reality, that human beings are both vulnerable and glorious. It is God who plants the garden in readiness for the human beings, and they who are entrusted with the care of creation. Our reading also offers the opening verses of a second symbolic story, the story of the loss of the garden of God. The origin of evil is mysterious and symbolised by the snake which successfully tempts the woman and man to violate the limits laid down by God. There are limits to the freedom of choice given to human beings, and the violation of these limits brings consequences. The human couple become aware of good and evil, and hurriedly sew fig leaves to hide their shame. The two stories, of creation and sin, set the scene for history, both biblical and secular.

> **Psalm 51 (50)** This penitential psalm, known as the *Miserere* from its opening words 'have mercy', is fitting after the story of the sin of our first parents, and prepares us for Paul's assertion that 'everyone has sinned'.

A reading from the letter of St Paul to the Romans (5:12-19)

Therefore, just as through one man sin *came into the world*, and through sin death, and thus death has spread through the whole human race in so far as everyone has sinned – sin already existed in the world before there was any law, but sin is not reckoned when there is no law. Nonetheless death reigned over all from Adam to Moses, even over those whose sin was not after the model of Adam's transgression, who prefigured the one who was to come.

Yet the free gift is not like the offence. If death came to many through the offence of one man, how much more plentiful has been the grace of God and the free gift in the love of the one man Jesus Christ coming to so many! Again, the gift is not like the effect of the one man who sinned. For the judgement after the one offence issued in condemnation, while the gift after many offences issued in justification. If it was by one man's offence that death came to reign through one man, how much more will those who receive the abundance of grace and the gift of righteousness reign through the one man Jesus Christ! Well then, as one man's offence brought condemnation to all, so one man's good act has brought justification and life to all. Just as by one man's disobedience many were made sinners, so by one man's obedience are many to be made righteous.

IN THIS DIFFICULT PASSAGE St Paul draws a parallel between Adam and Christ, and compares what they bring to the human race. As we were

FIRST WEEK IN LENT

reminded in the first reading today, Adam brings sin into the world. Paul tells us that sin spreads, 'in so far as everyone has sinned', and that death comes into the world through sin. But what Jesus brings is life. Paul uses various terms to describe the 'gift' brought by Jesus. While sin brings condemnation, the gift brings 'justification', 'abundance of grace', and 'the gift of righteousness'. Paul's profound reflection on the gift Jesus brings is the fruit of his encounter with Christ, his love of Christ, and his years of preaching about the 'mystery' of Christ.

A reading from the holy gospel according to Matthew (4:1-11)

Then Jesus was led by the Spirit out into the desert to be put to the test by the devil. He fasted for forty days and forty nights, after which he was hungry, and the tempter came and said to him, 'If you are Son of God, tell these stones to turn into loaves.' But he replied, 'It is written:

A human lives not on bread alone
but on every word that comes from the mouth of God.'

Then the devil took him to the holy city and set him on the parapet of the Temple, and said to him, 'If you are Son of God throw yourself down, for it is written:

He will give his angels orders about you,
and they will carry you in their hands
in case you trip on a stone.'

Jesus said to him, 'It is also written:
Do not put the Lord your God to the test.'

Next, taking him to a very high mountain, the devil showed him all the kingdoms of the world and their glory. And he said to him, 'These shall all be yours if you fall at my feet and worship me.' Then Jesus replied, 'Away with you, Satan! For it is written:

The Lord your God shall you worship
and him alone shall you serve.'

Then the devil left him, and see, angels appeared and looked after him.

IT IS FITTING THAT the gospel for this first Sunday of Lent speaks of the forty days of Jesus in the desert, which inspired the Christian Lent. The evangelist

Matthew elaborates the fundamental tradition found in Mark, that Jesus was tested by the devil. There is a catechesis here about sin, and its insidiousness. The devil attacks Jesus in his time of weakness, as he suffers the hunger of forty days' fasting. He then abuses the human craving for recognition and praise, urging Jesus to do something spectacular to show he is better than others. To add strength to this temptation the devil also uses Scripture, but this temptation also fails. The final temptation is about power, and the compromise needed to obtain it. Jesus does not dialogue with Satan, but simply quotes from the Scriptures. The power of God's word prevails.

Was Jesus really tempted?
For those who are crushed by the temptations of pleasure, prestige and power, we pray.

FIRST SUNDAY OF LENT – YEAR B

A reading from the book of Genesis (9:8-15)

God spoke as follows to Noah and his sons with him, 'I am now establishing my covenant with you and with your descendants to come, and with every living creature that is with you: birds, cattle and every wild animal with you; everything that came out of the ark, every living thing on earth. And I establish my covenant with you: that never again shall all living things be destroyed by the waters of a flood, nor shall there ever again be a flood to devastate the earth.' God said, 'This is the sign of the covenant which I now make between myself and you and every living creature with you for all ages to come: I now set my bow in the clouds and it will be the sign of the covenant between me and the earth. When I gather the clouds over the earth and the bow appears in the clouds, I shall recall the covenant between myself and you and every living creature, all living things, and never again will the waters become a flood to destroy all living things. When the bow is in the clouds I shall see it and call to mind the eternal covenant between God and every living creature on earth, all living things.' God said to Noah, 'This is the sign of the covenant I have established between myself and all living things on earth.'

FIRST WEEK IN LENT

THE FLOOD TAKES UP four chapters of the book of Genesis (chapters 6-9). The story of the Flood, an ancient traditional theme found in many civilisations, is in the Hebrew Bible an attempt to explain the devastating natural disasters human beings and the whole of creation periodically experience. They cannot be God's will, and therefore, or so it seems, must be caused by human sin (6:5-7). Our passage tells of the resolution of the crisis and the establishment of the 'covenant' (*berit*), the solemn bond between God and human beings. This is the first time in the Scriptures that the term is used to denote the relationship between God and creation. The word appears seven times in verses 8-17, indicating completeness and the perfection of God's new initiative, which is celebrated by the wonderful natural phenomenon of the rainbow. God is committed to the well-being of creation, both human beings, the animals, and the natural world. The 'covenant' confirms this. It is human abuse that undermines the rainbow beauty of God's work.

> **Psalm 25 (24)** Focus on the covenant continues. The psalm expresses in a fresh way the message of the story of the Flood. All the ways of the Lord are steadfast love towards the covenant partners. God's mercy reaches back in history and forward into the future.

A reading from the first letter of St Peter (3:18-22)

Christ himself suffered once and for all for sins, the righteous for the unrighteous, to lead you to God. He was put to death in the body; he was raised to life in the spirit, in which he also went and made a proclamation to the spirits in prison. They had refused to believe long ago, while God patiently waited, in the days of Noah when the ark was being built, in which only a few, that is eight souls, were saved through water. Baptism which this prefigured now saves you, not the removal of physical dirt but the pledge to God of a good conscience through the resurrection of Jesus Christ, who is at the right hand of God, having entered heaven with angels, authorities and powers subject to him.

DEATH AND LIFE ARE the focus here. Jesus was put to death in the body, and raised in the spirit. The 'proclamation to the spirits in prison' is obscure, but might be pointing to the releasing from death through the resurrection of Jesus of people of earlier generations. Salvation from the waters of the flood becomes in its turn a pointer to the Baptism 'which now saves you', and gives access to the new covenant, brought by Jesus Christ.

A reading from the holy gospel according to Mark (1:12-15)

And at once the Spirit drove him into the desert and he was in the desert for forty days, being put to the test by Satan. He was with the wild animals, and the angels looked after him.

After John had been arrested, Jesus went into Galilee, proclaiming the gospel from God and saying, 'The time is fulfilled, and the kingdom of God has drawn near. Repent and believe in the gospel.'

FROM THE GOSPEL OF Mark, the earliest gospel, this is the original and terse report of Christ's being tested. It is as if the evangelist is embarrassed even to mention it. The Spirit 'drives' Jesus to this encounter. Like Moses and Elijah, he must spend forty days in the desert. Biblical tradition reports that Moses was forty days in God's presence on Sinai (Exodus 24). Elijah travelled for forty days to the holy mountain (1 Kings 19). No details of the temptations are provided in this stark account, but the accompanying statements proclaim Jesus as the new Adam, for he is at peace with all creation, and is close to God, and served by God's angels. Jesus is, as St Paul explains at length in Romans 5, the Adam who through fidelity to God brings grace, life and salvation. Despite being tempted, Jesus chose to be faithful.

Jesus is like us in all things but sin. Jesus resists the lure of Satan. For those who work to combat the exploitation of creation, we pray.

FIRST SUNDAY OF LENT – YEAR C

A reading from the book of Deuteronomy (26:4-10)

Moses said to the people: 'The priest will take the basket from your hand and lay it before the altar of the LORD your God. In the presence of the LORD your God, you will then pronounce these words, "My father was a wandering Aramaean; he went down to Egypt, few in number, and stayed there; there he became a great, powerful and numerous nation. The Egyptians ill-treated us, they oppressed us and inflicted harsh slavery on us. But we called on the LORD, God of our ancestors. The LORD heard our voice and saw our misery, our toil and our oppression. The LORD brought us out of Egypt with mighty hand and outstretched arm, with great terror, and with signs and wonders. He brought us here and has given us this land, a land flowing with milk and honey. So I now bring the first-fruits of the soil that you, LORD , have given me." You will then set it down before the LORD your God, and prostrate yourself in the presence of the LORD your God.'

THE RITUAL OF PRESENTING to God the first fruits of the harvest is spelt out here. As the person offering approaches the priest, he makes a declaration about the acts of God for Israel from the patriarchs until the entry into the promised land. The reference to the 'wandering Aramaean' may well be to Jacob, who spent years in the ancestral land of Aram after his rift with Esau (Genesis 28). The declaration recalls that the Israelites have been delivered from slavery in Egypt and brought to a 'fruitful' land, where 'milk and honey' flow. In gratitude the person offers the first fruits of 'the soil you have given me'. The confession of God's good deeds for Israel is followed by an offering to God.

> **Psalm 91 (90)** This psalm prepares us for the gospel of the temptations, during which the devil uses this text to ensnare Jesus, and assure him of God's protection if he hurls himself off the temple parapet: 'his angels will keep you in all your ways'.

A reading from the letter of St Paul to the Romans (10:8-13)

Scripture says: *The word is near to you; it is in your mouth and in your heart* (that is, the word of the faith which we proclaim). If you declare with your mouth that Jesus is Lord, and if you believe in your heart that God raised him from the dead, you will be saved. Belief with the heart leads to righteousness, and confession with the lips leads to salvation.

Scripture says: *No one who believes in him will be brought to disgrace,* for there is no distinction between Jew and Greek: the same Lord is the Lord of all, generous to all who call on him, for *everyone who calls on the name of the Lord will be saved.*

AFTER THE DECLARATION OF faith in the previous reading St Paul gives us the essence of the Christian creed, that Jesus is Lord, and that God raised him from the dead. Belief 'with the heart' brings 'righteousness', and confession 'with the lips' brings 'salvation'. These gifts are given to all who believe, Jew and gentile alike, for God is 'generous' in mercy. Paul ends the passage with a quotation from the second part of Isaiah, from the prophet who looked forward to universal salvation. The words Paul quotes from this part of Scripture are fulfilled with the coming of Jesus Christ, the Lord.

A reading from the holy gospel according to Luke (4:1-13)

Filled with the Holy Spirit, Jesus left the Jordan and was led by the Spirit into the desert, for forty days being put to the test by the devil. During that time he ate nothing at all and when they were over he was hungry. Then the devil said to him, 'If you are Son of God, tell this stone to become a loaf.' But Jesus replied to him, 'Scripture says:

A human does not live on bread alone.'

Then, leading him to a height, the devil showed him in a moment of time all the kingdoms of the world and said to him, 'I will give you all this power and their splendour, for it has been handed over to me, and I give it to anyone I wish. If you, then, worship me, it shall all be yours.' But Jesus answered him, 'It is written:

You shall worship the Lord your God, him alone shall you serve.'

Then he led him to Jerusalem and set him on the parapet of the Temple and said to him, 'If you are Son of God throw yourself down from here, for it is written:

He has given his angels orders about you, to guard you, and that,
They will carry you in their arms in case you trip on a stone.'

But Jesus answered him, 'It is said:

Do not put the Lord your God to the test.'

Having finished every way of putting him to the test, the devil left him, until the opportune moment.

FIRST WEEK IN LENT

THE ACCOUNT OF THE temptations in the gospel of Luke is, like Matthew's account, developed from the brief reference in Mark's gospel. The texts of Scripture used by Jesus, and by Satan, are the same. The temptations concern pleasure, prestige and power, but the order of the temptations is changed. In Luke the final temptation is that Jesus should demonstrate his status by throwing himself off the parapet of the Temple. At this point, as in Matthew, Satan quotes from Psalm 91, that God's angels will protect Jesus. The positioning of this Jerusalem temptation as the final one matches Luke's emphasis on the role of Jerusalem in the gospel story of Luke, which began with the vision of the priest Zechariah in the temple in Jerusalem, and will end with the apostles gathering for prayer in the temple after the ascension of the Lord. Luke's account concludes with an ominous reference to the return of the devil at the 'opportune moment', and in 22:3, as the story of the Passion begins, Luke will indeed maintain that Satan 'entered into Judas'.

How can I derive strength and encouragement from the Scriptures?
For those who put temptation in the way of the innocent, we pray.

MONDAY OF FIRST WEEK IN LENT

A reading from the book of Leviticus (19:1-2,11-18)

The LORD spoke to Moses and said, 'Speak to the whole community of Israelites and say, "Be holy, for I, the LORD your God, am holy.

' "You shall not steal, nor deal deceitfully or fraudulently with your fellow-citizen. You shall not swear by my name with intent to deceive and thus profane the name of your God. I am the LORD.

' "You shall not defraud your neighbour. You shall not steal. You shall not keep back the labourer's wage until next morning. You shall not curse the dumb or put an obstacle in the way of the blind, but you shall fear your God. I am the LORD.

' "You shall not do evil in administering justice. You shall neither be partial to the poor nor overawed by the great, but shall administer justice to your fellow-citizen justly. You shall not go about slandering your own family, nor will you endanger your neighbour's life. I am the LORD.

' "You shall not have hatred in your heart for any of your kin. You shall reprove your neighbour firmly and so avoid taking the guilt upon yourself. You shall not exact vengeance on, or bear any sort of grudge against, the members of your race, but shall love your neighbour as yourself. I am the Lord."'

AN IMPORTANT SECTION OF the book of Leviticus (17-26) is known as 'the Holiness Code' and this reading is taken from these chapters. The holiness of God requires that God's people too be holy. Our passage is punctuated with the fourfold declaration from the holy God: 'I am the Lord'. Holiness requires honest and respectful behaviour towards the neighbour, which is spelt out in a multitude of ways. Stealing, deceit, and swearing false oaths recall the commandments of the Decalogue (Exodus 20). Keeping back the wages of the worker, and abuse of the dumb and the blind are condemned, while the 'fear' of the Lord is encouraged. The proper administration of justice rules out partiality in judgement. 'Hatred in your heart' and 'vengeance' are replaced by the final command: 'you shall love your neighbour as yourself'.

> **Psalm 19 (18)** The psalm renews the focus on the Law of the Lord, which brings life and wisdom, joy and light. The 'fear of the Lord' is not something negative, but appropriate awe in the presence of a God of justice and love.

A reading from the holy gospel according to Matthew (25:31-46)

Jesus said to his disciples: 'When the Son of man comes in his glory, escorted by all the angels, then he will take his seat on his throne of glory. All nations will be assembled before him and he will separate them from one another as the shepherd separates sheep from goats. He will place the sheep on his right hand and the goats on his left. Then the King will say to those on his right hand, "Come, you that are blessed by my Father, inherit the kingdom prepared for you since the foundation of the world. For I was hungry and you gave me food, I was thirsty and you gave me drink, I was a stranger and you welcomed me, needing clothes and you clothed me, sick and you visited me, in prison and you came to see me." Then the righteous will say to him in reply, "Lord, when did we see you hungry and feed you, or thirsty and give you drink? When did we see you a stranger and welcome you, needing clothes and we clothed you? When did we see you sick or in prison and go to you?" And the King will answer, "Amen I say to you, in so far as you did this to one of the least of these brothers or sisters of mine, you did it to me." Then he will say to those on his left hand, "Go away from me, accursed, to the eternal fire prepared for the devil and his angels. For I was hungry and you did not give me food, I was thirsty and you did not give me anything to drink, I was a stranger and you did not welcome me, needing clothes and you never clothed me, sick and in prison and you did not visit me." Then they in their turn will ask, "Lord, when did we see you hungry or thirsty, a stranger or needing clothes, sick or in prison, and did not come to your aid?" Then he will answer, "Amen I say to you, in so far as you neglected to do this to one of the least of these, you neglected to do it to me." And they will go away to eternal punishment, and the righteous to eternal life.'

THE PARABLE OF THE sheep and the goats is the last part of the fifth and final major speech of Jesus in the gospel of Matthew, a speech which considers the future and the end. This 'last judgement' asks how we treat others, and in particular those in need. It is the gospel call to 'love your neighbour as yourself', with the significant change that 'all the nations' are included. Solidarity with the poor, the hungry and those on the margins is the fundamental criterion of the judgement. Every person is my brother or sister, and in each I serve Christ. The virtuous are amazed that they have served Christ in each person in need. The parable ends with the stark choice between 'eternal punishment' and 'eternal life'. It is not possible to reach eternal life without having reached out to brothers and sisters in need.

How can I serve Jesus in those I do not like?
For the needy who are noticed by no one, let us pray.

TUESDAY OF THE FIRST WEEK IN LENT

A reading from the book of Isaiah (55:10-11)
Thus says the Lord:
'For as the rain and the snow come down from the sky
and do not return before watering the earth,
fertilising it and making it germinate
to provide seed for the sower and food to eat,
so it is with the word that goes forth from my mouth:
it does not return to me unfulfilled
or before carrying out my purpose
and achieving what it was sent to do.'

THIS SHORT SAYING COMES towards the end of the chapters of the book of Isaiah (40-55) attributed to a prophet active in the Babylonian exile. This 'Second Isaiah' has often spoken about God's powerful word, and maintained that God declares beforehand what is to come about (42:9). God is more powerful and more compassionate than the false gods of the nations, and the word of this God 'stands firm for ever' (40:8).

> **Psalm 34 (33)** This psalm celebrates the God who hears and responds to prayer, especially the prayer of those in distress.

A reading from the holy gospel according to Matthew (6:7-15)
Jesus said to his disciples: 'In your prayers do not babble as gentiles do, for they think that by using many words they will make themselves heard. Do not be like them; your Father knows what you need before you ask him. Pray, then, like this:
  'Our Father in heaven,
  may your name be held holy,
  your kingdom come,
  your will be done, on earth as in heaven.

Give us today our daily bread.
And forgive us our debts,
as we have forgiven our debtors.
And do not put us to the test, but save us from the Evil One.

'For if you forgive others their failings, your heavenly Father will forgive you yours; but if you do not forgive others, your Father will not forgive your failings either.'

AT THE HEART OF THE Sermon on the Mount we read Matthew's version of the 'Lord's Prayer'. Jesus draws a contrast not with Jewish forms of prayer, which are in fact reflected here, but with the 'babbling' of the gentiles. Three petitions, concerning the name of God, the kingdom and the will of God, have us pray for the revelation of God's glory. Then we are directed to seek three things. 'Bread' for today and tomorrow represents every physical need. Forgiveness is repeatedly a concern in the Sermon on the Mount, and throughout Matthew's gospel, as in the parable of the unforgiving debtor (chapter 18). Finally, the Christian requests escape from the 'test', the time of trial (*peirasmos*), and deliverance from the Evil One (*poneros*). Christ's prayer strengthens the will and feeds the heart as we journey towards God.

Identify each of the petitions in the Our Father, and pray them separately.
For those who struggle to call God 'father', we pray.

WEDNESDAY OF THE FIRST WEEK IN LENT

A reading from the book of Jonah (3:1-10)

The word of the LORD came to Jonah a second time saying, 'Up! Go to Nineveh the great city and proclaim to it the message I tell you.' So Jonah set out and went to Nineveh according to the word of the LORD. Now Nineveh was a city great beyond compare; to cross it took three days. Jonah began by going a day's journey into the city and then proclaimed, 'Only forty days more and Nineveh will be overthrown.' And the people of Nineveh believed in God; they proclaimed a fast and put on sackcloth, from the greatest to the least. When the news reached the king of Nineveh, he rose from his throne, took off his robe, put on sackcloth and sat down in ashes. Then he had it proclaimed throughout Nineveh, by decree of the king and his nobles, as follows: 'No person or animal, herd or flock, shall eat anything; they shall not feed, nor shall they drink water. All must put on sackcloth and call on God with all their might; and let everyone renounce their evil ways and the violence that is in their hands. Who knows? Perhaps God will change his mind and relent and renounce his burning wrath so that we shall not perish.' God saw their efforts to renounce their evil ways. And God relented about the disaster which he had said he would to bring on them and did not bring it.

THE LORD HAD TO send Jonah twice. When first sent, Jonah refused and headed off in the opposite direction towards Tarshish, long associated with Spain (Jonah 1). God had to take extreme measures to bring this prophet back. Even now, called for a second time, Jonah is far from convinced he should preach to Nineveh, capital of the Assyrian empire, an arch-enemy of Israel. His preaching is just five words long in Hebrew (nine in our English translation). Jonah has only travelled one day into the city, which takes three days to cross, and God's work of conversion begins. It is the king of Nineveh, and his nobles, who grasp the urgency of the situation and preach to the people the message of repentance and divine mercy. The response of the people, and even of the animals, is to seek forgiveness. God's mercy averts 'disaster'. But Jonah remains stubbornly unconvinced and unrepentant (Jonah 4).

> **Psalm 51 (50)** Once more, for the third time this Lent, we pray this psalm of mercy. A humble and contrite heart is welcomed by God, who offers pardon to those who ask for it. The people of Nineveh know what this means.

A reading from the holy gospel according to Luke (11:29-32)

The crowds got even bigger and Jesus began to say, 'This is an evil generation; it asks for a sign. The only sign it will be given is the sign of Jonah. For just as Jonah became a sign to the people of Nineveh, so will the Son of man be a sign to this generation. At the judgement the Queen of the South will stand up with the people of this generation and condemn them, because she came from the ends of the earth to hear the wisdom of Solomon; and, look, there is something greater than Solomon here. At the judgement the men of Nineveh will take their stand and condemn it, because they repented at Jonah's proclamation; and, look, there is something greater than Jonah here.'

THE CONSTANT QUEST FOR a 'sign' shows an unwillingness to take Jesus seriously and to acknowledge the power of his words and actions. Jesus is the real sign. The people could learn from the Queen of Sheba, who travelled hundreds of miles to find the wisdom of king Solomon (1 Kings 10). They could learn from the Ninevites, led by their astute king, who understood God's mercy, and changed their ways (Jonah 3). And Jesus insists that there is something greater than Solomon or Jonah here.

Do we still look for signs, even though Jesus Christ speaks to us and acts for us?
For the humility to learn from others, we pray.

THURSDAY OF THE FIRST WEEK IN LENT

A reading from the book of Esther (4:17)

Queen Esther also took refuge with the Lord in the mortal peril which had overtaken her. She besought the Lord God of Israel in these words:
> 'My Lord, our King, the only one,
> come to my help, for I am alone
> and have no helper but you,
> and am about to take my life in my hands.
> I have been taught from my earliest years
> in my father's clan,
> that you, Lord, chose Israel out of all the nations,
> and our ancestors out of all their forebears

to be your eternal heritage;
and that you have treated them as you promised.
Remember, Lord; reveal yourself
in this time of our distress.
Give me courage,
King of gods and master of all power.
Put persuasive words into my mouth
when I face the lion;
change his heart into hatred for our enemy
so that he and all like him may be brought to their end.
Save us by your hand, and come to my help,
for I am alone and have no one but you, Lord.'

THE BOOK OF ESTHER tells the story of a beautiful Jewish queen who faces a terrible dilemma. She is forbidden to enter the presence of her husband the king uninvited, but must approach 'the lion' because of the threatened genocide of her people. This prayer, in which Esther desperately seeks strength from the Lord, is an addition in the Greek language to the Hebrew book of Esther. In it Esther recalls God's choice of Israel and fidelity to the covenant. This gives her courage in the predicament in which she is now. The prayer arises from profound meditation on the courage of this Jewish woman, who, as the story goes on to report, wins freedom and reprieve for her people.

> **Psalm 138 (137)** This psalm expresses thanks for an answer to prayer, and so is fitting after the reading about Esther. The faithfulness and love of God are eternal.

A reading from the holy gospel according to Matthew (7:7-12)

Jesus said to his disciples: 'Ask, and it will be given to you; search, and you will find; knock, and the door will be opened to you. Everyone who asks receives; everyone who searches finds; to everyone who knocks the door will be opened. Is there anyone among you who, if your child asks for bread, would give a stone? Or, if your child asks for a fish, would give a snake? If you, then, evil as you are, know how to give your children what is good, how much more will your Father in heaven give good things to those who ask him!

'So always treat others as you would like them to treat you; that is the Law and the Prophets.'

THE THEME OF PRAYER IS taken up again in another excerpt from the Sermon on the Mount. We are not dealing with a specific danger, but with the general needs of human beings, often expressed in prayer. Jesus responds by saying that, if parents normally care for their children and provide what they need, it is clear that 'your Father in heaven' will not fail to respond. We may not receive exactly what we ask for, for God knows what is for our good better than we ourselves do. The gospel passage concludes with the 'golden rule' – 'treat others as you would like them to treat you' – which is found also outside the confines of Judaism and Christianity. For Jesus love of brothers and sisters sums up the Law and the Prophets.

Pray for what God wants, not for what we want.
For people who only pray when they are desperate, let us pray.

FRIDAY OF THE FIRST WEEK IN LENT

A reading from the prophet Ezekiel (18:21-28)

Thus says the Lord: 'If the wicked, however, renounces all the sins he has committed, respects my laws and is law-abiding and righteous, he will most certainly live; he will not die. None of the crimes he committed will be remembered against him from then on; he will most certainly live because of his righteous actions. Would I take pleasure in the death of the wicked – declares the Lord GOD – and not prefer to see him renounce his wickedness and live?

'But if the righteous abandons righteousness and does wrong, copying all the loathsome practices of the wicked, is he to live? All his righteous actions will be forgotten from then on; for the infidelity of which he is guilty and the sin which he has committed, he will most certainly die.

'But you say, "What the LORD does is unjust." Now listen, House of Israel: is what I do unjust? Is it not what you do that is unjust? When the righteous abandons righteousness and does wrong and dies, he dies because of the wrong which he himself has done. Similarly, when the wicked abandons wickedness to become law-abiding and righteous, he saves his own life. Having chosen to renounce all his previous crimes, he will most certainly live: he will not die.'

THIS SECTION OF MORAL teaching of the prophet Ezekiel begins and ends on an optimistic note. It is possible for human beings to change from wickedness to goodness, and God welcomes this change. In the heart of the reading, however, lies the warning that the converse is also true, for human beings can move from goodness to wickedness, so that their goodness will be forgotten. There is always the opportunity to change. God treats a person for what that person is, not what they may have been in the past. God, who is supremely just, yearns for the sinner to 'renounce his wickedness and live', taking pleasure not in death but in life. The good God awaits the goodness which every person can freely give.

> **Psalm 130 (129)** This psalm, the De profundis, is traditionally prayed for the dead. It is chosen here to resonate with the possibility of change through the mercy of God, with whom is found forgiveness and fullness of redemption.

A reading from the holy gospel according to Matthew (5:20-26)

Jesus said to his disciples: 'If your righteousness does not surpass that of the scribes and Pharisees, you will never get into the kingdom of Heaven.

'You have heard that it was said to our ancestors, "*You shall not murder*"; and whoever murders must answer for it before the court. But I say this to you, anyone who is angry with a brother or sister will answer for it before the court; anyone who calls a brother or sister "idiot" will answer for it before the assembly; and anyone who calls a brother or sister "fool" will answer for it in hell fire. So then, if you are offering your gift at the altar and there remember that your brother or sister has something against you, leave your gift there before the altar, go and first be reconciled with your brother or sister, and then come and offer your gift. Come to terms with your opponent in good time while you are still on the way to the court together, or your opponent may hand you over to the judge and the judge to the attendant, and you will be thrown into prison. Amen I say to you, you will not get out till you have paid the last coin.'

JESUS BRINGS A NEW kind of righteousness, a new kind of justice (*dikaiosyne*), which surpasses that of the scribes and Pharisees. In a series of six contrasts, known as 'antitheses', in the Sermon on the Mount, Jesus offers the challenge of a broader justice. The antitheses are punctuated with 'You have heard it said', and 'I say this to you.' Jesus, the new Moses, deepens the traditional teaching. In this first antithesis Jesus makes clear that there are to be no half measures, no half goodness, but wholeheartedness. External acts are one thing, but God sees and judges the heart. Anger and hatred against brother or sister are on the same level as murder. Reconciliation with the brother or sister must always be the first concern, and does as much good to the one who offers it as to the one to whom it is offered.

While Ezekiel assures us that God welcomes change for the good,
    Jesus exemplifies what such change could look like.
For the grace of a new heart, we pray.

SATURDAY OF THE FIRST WEEK IN LENT

A reading from the book of Deuteronomy (26:16-19)
Moses said to the people: 'Today the Lord your God commands you to observe these laws and customs; you shall keep and observe them with all your heart and with all your soul. Today you have brought the Lord your God to declare that he will be your God, and that you will walk in his ways, keep his statutes, his commandments, his customs, and listen to his voice. And today the Lord has brought you to declare that you

will be his treasured people – as he has said – and that you will keep all his commandments; then for praise and renown and splendour, he will raise you higher than every other nation he has made, and you will be a people holy to the Lord, as he has promised.'

THIS SOLEMN READING INVITES a renewal of the covenant between Israel and God, and is punctuated with three uses of the word 'today'. At Moses' bidding the people of Israel renew their solemn commitment to the Law of the Lord, with its 'statutes', 'commandments' and 'customs', to be kept and observed 'with all your heart' and 'with all your soul'. The people have 'brought the Lord to declare' that 'he will be your God'. And the Lord has 'brought you to declare' that 'you are his treasured people'. This amounts to a renewal of the covenant, reflecting the basic formula 'I will be your God, and you will be my people' (Jeremiah 31:33). They are committed once more to be a people 'holy to the Lord'.

> **Psalm 119 (118)** Psalm 119 is a magnificent celebration of the Law, source of happiness, and is constructed as an 'acrostic', where every stanza begins with a subsequent letter of the Hebrew alphabet.

A reading from the holy gospel according to Matthew (5:43-48)

Jesus said to his disciples: 'You have heard how it was said, "*You shall love your neighbour* and hate your enemy". But I say this to you, love your enemies and pray for those who persecute you; so that you may be children of your Father in heaven, for he causes his sun to rise on the evil as well as the good, and sends down rain on the righteous and the wicked alike. For if you love those who love you, what reward do you have? Do not even the tax collectors do as much? And if you save your greetings for your brothers and sisters, are you doing anything exceptional? Do not even the gentiles do as much? You must therefore be perfect, as your heavenly Father is perfect.'

THIS IS THE SIXTH and final 'antithesis' from the Sermon on the Mount. Yesterday we heard the new ruling of Jesus to avoid all anger and aggression against others. Today the command is to love not only the neighbour, but the enemy too. Christians should both love the enemy and pray for the persecutor. The goodness of the creator God , who provides sun and rain for all, is in this way imitated by the children of God. The standard is higher than that practised by tax collectors and gentiles, even though their conduct might sometimes be exemplary. This final antithesis points most clearly to the newer and deeper justice which God invites (Matthew 5:20). There is nothing greater than to seek to imitate the all-embracing love of God. Jesus concludes: 'You are to be perfect (*teleioi*), as your heavenly Father is perfect'.

Am I ready to pursue new standards of goodness, inspired by the wisdom of Jesus?
Pray for the desire to be 'perfect', without embarrassment, and the wisdom to know what it means to be 'holy'.

Second Week in Lent

SECOND SUNDAY OF LENT – YEAR A

A reading from the book of Genesis (12:1-4)

The Lord said to Abram, 'Leave your country, your kindred and your father's house for a country that I shall show you; and I shall make you into a great nation, I shall bless you and make your name famous; you are to be a blessing!

'I shall bless those who bless you,
and curse those who curse you,
and all clans on earth
will bless themselves by you.'
So Abram went as the Lord told him.

THE STORY OF ABRAM, later to be called Abraham (Genesis 17), begins with the command of the Lord that he should set out on a journey. Abram promptly obeys. In Genesis 1 God blesses both human beings and the fish of the sea. The story of Abram, with which salvation history begins in Genesis 12, also announces blessings. Guided only by the word of God, Abram is to leave what he has and trust in God alone. God will bless him, and bless those who bless him, so that all the nations will bless themselves by him. This image of harmony throughout the earth is built on the faith of Abram in God who provides for all. The story of God and of the people of God is essentially a story of blessing.

> **Psalm 33 (32)** As Abraham knew, the word of God is to be trusted. Abraham, who showed reverence for God, knows God as 'help' and 'shield'.

A reading from the second letter of St Paul to Timothy (1:8-10)

Share in my hardships for the sake of the gospel, relying on the power of God, who has saved us and called us with a holy calling – not because of anything we ourselves had done but for his own purpose and by his own grace, granted to us, in Christ Jesus, before the beginning of time; but revealed only by the appearing of our Saviour Christ Jesus, who both abolished death and brought to light life and immortality through the gospel.

THE CHRISTIAN IS CALLED to share in the suffering which preaching the gospel brings, for God has both saved us and called us, with a call which does not rely on any good deeds we have done but is a gift of grace. The gift, prepared from long ago, is revealed by the 'appearing' *(epifaneia)* of the Saviour, who destroys death, and brings life and immortality. The gospel proclaims a free gift of God revealed in the coming of 'our Saviour Christ Jesus'.

A reading from the holy gospel according to Matthew (17:1-9)

Jesus took with him Peter and James and his brother John and led them up a high mountain on their own. In their presence he was transfigured: his face shone like the sun and his clothes became as dazzling as light. And suddenly Moses and Elijah appeared to them, talking with him. Then Peter spoke to Jesus, saying, 'Lord, it is wonderful for us to be here; if you want me to, I will make three shelters here, one for you, one for Moses and one for Elijah.' He was still speaking when suddenly a bright cloud covered them with shadow, and suddenly from the cloud there came a voice which said, 'This is my Son, the Beloved; he enjoys my favour. Listen to him.' When they heard this, the disciples fell on their faces, overcome with fear. But Jesus came up and touched them, saying, 'Stand up, do not be afraid.' And when they raised their eyes they saw no one but Jesus himself alone.

THE STORY OF THE transfiguration is told in the gospels of Matthew, Mark and Luke, in a broadly similar way. To grasp the significance of the story we must bear in mind that it happens just as Jesus prepares to journey to Jerusalem, and as he speaks to his disciples for the first time of his coming death and resurrection.

Moses and Elijah, who appear in the scene, are remembered as having conquered death. The testimony of Scripture is that the grave of Moses was never found (Deuteronomy 34), and that Elijah was taken up in a chariot to heaven (2 Kings 2). These traditions point us towards the idea of resurrection. In the strange experience of the transfiguration three chosen disciples are given a glimpse of resurrection glory. Meanwhile we are bidden by the voice of God to 'listen' to Jesus.

How does this story prepare us for the Cross?
For all who today need courage to face death, their own, or the death of another, we pray.

SECOND SUNDAY OF LENT – YEAR B

A reading from the book of Genesis (22:1-2, 9-13, 15-18)

It happened some time later that God put Abraham to the test. 'Abraham, Abraham!' he called. 'Here I am,' he replied. God said, 'Take your son, your only son, Isaac whom you love, and go to the land of Moriah, and there you shall offer him as a burnt offering on one of the mountains which I shall point out to you.'

When they arrived at the place that God had indicated to him, Abraham built an altar there, and arranged the wood. Then he bound his son Isaac and put him on the altar on top of the wood. Abraham reached out his hand and took the knife to kill his son. But the angel of the Lord called to him from heaven. 'Abraham, Abraham!' he said. 'Here I am,' he replied. He said, 'Do not raise your hand against the boy or do anything to him, for now I know you fear God. You have not refused me your own beloved son.' Then looking up, Abraham saw a ram caught by its horns in a bush. Abraham went and took the ram and offered it as a burnt offering in place of his son.

The angel of the Lord called Abraham a second time from heaven. 'I swear by my own self, the Lord declares, that because you have done this, because you have not refused me your own beloved son, I will shower blessings on you and make your descendants as numerous as the stars of heaven and the grains of sand on the seashore. Your descendants will gain possession of the gates of their enemies. All nations on earth will bless themselves by your descendants, because you have obeyed my command.'

A MAJOR FEATURE OF the story of Abraham in the book of Genesis is that God repeatedly promises that he and his wife Sarah will have a son. Isaac is eventually born when both parents are elderly (Genesis 21). Naturally Abraham is horrified when he is led to believe that God is asking him to take his son, 'his only son, Isaac whom he loves', to be offered as a burnt offering on a mountain God will show him. Abraham, nevertheless, complies and makes the journey to Moriah, the mountain indicated by God, traditionally identified with Mount Sion, on which the Temple would be built. On arrival and, after all the preparations have been made to sacrifice the boy, God intervenes to stop Abraham from killing the child. Abraham's willingness to obey shows that he truly 'fears God', for he has not refused to offer back to God the greatest gift God has given him, the son for Sarah and Abraham so long awaited, the child of the promise. The story concludes with a solemn restatement of the promise by God: Abraham's descendants will be as numerous as the stars and as the sand on the seashore.

> **Psalm 116 (115)** The psalm speaks of the promised 'land of the living', held out to Abraham, and fully revealed by Christ.

A reading from the letter of St Paul to the Romans (8:31-34)

If God is for us, who can be against us? Since he did not spare his own Son, but gave him up for the sake of us all, will he not with him give us everything else? Who can bring a charge against those whom God has chosen? It is God who justifies; who can condemn? Jesus Christ who died, or rather was raised up, who is also at the right hand of God and who intercedes for us?

THE EIGHTH CHAPTER OF the Letter to the Romans is a celebration of salvation in Christ. In a series of rhetorical questions St Paul expresses his amazement at God's plan for salvation. God did not keep back his own Son, but gave him up for the salvation of the human race. It follows that no one can condemn those whom God has chosen, and least of all Jesus, who now sits at God's right hand. To appreciate all this we need a deeper grasp of God's holiness, God's justice and God's love.

A reading from the holy gospel according to Mark (9:2-10)

Jesus took with him Peter and James and John and led them up a high mountain on their own by themselves. In their presence he was transfigured: his clothes became brilliantly white, whiter than any earthly bleacher could make them. Elijah appeared to them with Moses; and they were talking to Jesus. Then Peter spoke to Jesus, 'Rabbi,' he said, 'it is wonderful for us to be here; so let us make three shelters, one for you, one for Moses and one for Elijah.' He did not know what to say; they were so frightened. And a cloud came, covering them in shadow; and from the cloud came a voice, 'This is my Son, the Beloved. Listen to him.' Then suddenly, when they looked round, they saw no one with them any more but only Jesus.

As they were coming down from the mountain he instructed them to tell no one what they had seen, except when the Son of man had risen from the dead. And they kept the matter to themselves, though they puzzled what 'rising from the dead' could mean.

AS IN THE OTHER synoptic gospels Mark positions the story of the transfiguration at the time when Jesus is beginning the fateful journey to Jerusalem, and has spoken about his coming death and resurrection. Mark gives an honest account of the journey of faith of the disciples of Jesus, not concealing their frequent blunders. At the climax of the transfiguration story in all three synoptic gospels Peter blurts out 'it is wonderful for us to be here.' Only in Mark does the evangelist underline the gaucheness of this remark by speaking of the fear of the disciples. For Mark Peter 'did not know what to say; they were so frightened'. The cloud and the divine voice add to the mystery. Mark also honestly reports that the disciples struggled with the idea of 'rising from the dead'.

How much do the disciples learn from the transfiguration experience?
Pray for those who prefer their own comfort to honestly facing the problems of life.

SECOND SUNDAY OF LENT – YEAR C

A reading from the book of Genesis (15:5-12, 17-18)

Then taking Abram outside, he said, 'Look up at the sky and count the stars if you can. Just so will your descendants be,' he told him. Abram put his faith in the Lord and this was reckoned to him as righteousness.

He then said to him, 'I am the Lord who brought you out of Ur of the Chaldaeans to give you this country as your possession.' Abram replied, 'Lord God, how can I know that I shall possess it?' He said to him, 'Bring me a three-year-old heifer, a three-year-old she-goat, a three-year-old ram, a turtledove and a young pigeon.' He brought him all these, split the animals down the middle and placed each half opposite the other; but the birds he did not divide. And when birds of prey swooped down on the carcasses, Abram drove them off.

Now, as the sun was on the point of setting, a deep sleep fell on Abram, and a deep, dark dread descended on him. When the sun had set and it was dark, there appeared a smoking firepot and a flaming torch passing between the animals' pieces. That day the Lord made a covenant with Abram in these terms:

'To your descendants I give this country,
from the River of Egypt to the Great River, the River Euphrates.'

THIS MYSTERIOUS ACCOUNT SIGNALS the making of a covenant between God and Abram. The faith of Abram was apparent at the beginning of his story when he was willing to leave his home to travel to a new land. His faith is emphasised again here, as he trusts God's promise of numerous descendants. This faith was considered as 'righteousness', and will be important for St Paul in his exploration of the nature of faith (Romans 4). The ancient ritual of sacrifice performed here was used to ratify covenants, and is referred

SECOND WEEK IN LENT

to in Jeremiah 34. The atmosphere is dark and threatening as a 'deep sleep' falls on Abram and a 'dark dread'. His vision of the 'smoking firepot' and the 'flaming torch' are symbols of the divine presence as God forges a covenant with him. The words of God again promise descendants and spell out the vast extensions of the land.

> **Psalm 27 (26)** The psalm promises the gift of the Lord's goodness 'in the land of the living'.

A reading from the letter of St Paul to the Philippians (3:17-4:1)

Brothers and sisters, be united in imitating me. Look towards those who act according to the example you have from me. For there are many people of whom I have often warned you, and now I warn you again with tears, who behave as enemies of Christ's cross. Their end is destruction; their god is the stomach; their glory is in their shame, since their minds are set on earthly things. But our citizenship is in heaven and from there we are expecting a Saviour, the Lord Jesus Christ, who will transform this wretched body of ours into the mould of his glorious body, through the working of the power which he has, even to make all things subject to him.

So then, my brothers and sisters, dear friends whom I miss, my joy and my crown; hold firm in the Lord, dear friends, in this way.

ST PAUL HAD A particular affection for the Christians of Philippi. This was the first place he visited on crossing from Asia to Europe (Acts 16), and he founded the church in that place. Now however these Christians are faced with a choice, and Paul is profoundly upset by the situation. They are being lured by people called by Paul 'the enemies of the cross of Christ' to conform to the requirements of Judaism, circumcision in particular. Paul warns them against 'earthly things', and that they should not give up the freedom they have received. Christians have a different prospect, for their 'citizenship is in heaven'. The Lord Jesus, at his coming, will transform 'this wretched body of ours' into a copy of 'his glorious body'. The Christian relies entirely on the power of Christ.

READING THE BIBLE THROUGH LENT

A reading from the holy gospel according to Luke (9:28-36)

Now about eight days after these sayings, taking Peter, John and James with him he went up the mountain to pray. And it happened that, as he was praying, the aspect of his face was changed and his clothing became dazzling white. And suddenly there were two men talking to him; they were Moses and Elijah appearing in glory, and they were speaking of his departure which he was to accomplish in Jerusalem. Peter and his companions were heavy with sleep, but when they were fully awake they saw his glory and the two men standing with him. As these were leaving him, Peter said to Jesus, 'Master, it is wonderful for us to be here; so let us make three shelters, one for you, one for Moses and one for Elijah,' not knowing what he was saying. While he was saying this, a cloud came and covered them with shadow; and as they went into the cloud the disciples were afraid. And a voice came from the cloud saying, 'This is my Son, the Chosen One. Listen to him.' And after the voice had spoken, Jesus was found alone. They themselves kept silence and, in those days, told no one what they had seen.

THE ACCOUNT OF THE transfiguration takes place as Jesus prepares to journey to Jerusalem. Luke tells us that 'the aspect of his face was changed'. He may well be alluding to the transformation in the face of Moses when he met the Lord (Exodus 34). Luke uniquely has Jesus in dialogue with Moses and Elijah about his 'departure' (*exodos*), which he was to accomplish in Jerusalem. Luke has Jesus solemnly begin this journey, his 'being taken up', later in the chapter, saying that he 'resolutely turned his face towards Jerusalem'. Luke also emphasises that the disciples saw the 'glory' of the Lord, an anticipation of his risen glory. Moses had been denied a vision of the glory of God (Exodus 33). In Luke's account the cloud fills the disciples with fear, and the words of God call Jesus 'son' and also 'chosen one'. Finally, Luke states that the disciples 'kept silent' about what they had seen, at least 'in those days'.

The words of God 'This is my Son' at the baptism and
    transfiguration of Jesus mark the two parts of the gospel story:
    the preaching of the kingdom, and the road to the Passion.
For those whose journey to God is particularly difficult, let us pray.

SECOND WEEK IN LENT

MONDAY OF THE SECOND WEEK IN LENT

A reading from the book of Daniel (9:4-10)

'I pleaded with the Lord my God and made this confession: "O my Lord, God great and to be feared, you keep the covenant and show faithful love towards those who love you and who observe your commandments: we have sinned, we have done wrong, we have acted wickedly, we have betrayed your commandments and rulings and turned away from them. We have not listened to your servants the prophets who spoke in your name to our kings, our chief men, our ancestors and all people of the land.

"Saving justice, Lord, is yours; we have only the look of shame we wear today, we, the people of Judah, the inhabitants of Jerusalem, the whole of Israel, near and far away, in every land to which you have dispersed us because of the treachery we have committed against you. To us, our kings, our chief men and our ancestors belongs the look of shame, O Lord, since we have sinned against you. It is for the Lord our God to have mercy and to forgive since we have betrayed him and have not listened to the voice of the Lord our God nor followed the laws he has given us through his servants the prophets."'

THIS PRAYER OF DANIEL, inspired by the reading of Scripture, is set during the Exile, but can be used in any situation of need. Daniel recalls the covenant love of God, and then repeatedly acknowledges the sin of the people. They admit: 'we have not listened to your servants the prophets who spoke in your name'. Disregarding God's word is the basis of all sin. God is a god of 'saving justice', but only 'shame' belongs to the people scattered 'near and far away'. Daniel prays fervently that God will show mercy and forgive.

> **Psalm 79 (78)** is a psalm of penitence, which reflects the statements in the prayer of Daniel.

A reading from the holy gospel according to Luke (6:36-38)

Jesus said to his disciples: 'Be compassionate just as your Father is compassionate. Do not judge, and you will not be judged; do not condemn, and you will not be condemned; forgive, and you will be forgiven. Give, and there will be gifts for you: a full measure, pressed down, shaken together, and overflowing, will be poured into your lap; because the standard you use will be the standard used for you.'

WHILE IN THE GOSPEL of Matthew, Jesus says 'Be perfect just as your heavenly Father is perfect', in Luke we learn what those words of Jesus might mean. Jesus insists here on being 'compassionate', a word which has a depth of feeling to it and a clear requirement of holiness and love. It is accompanied by four more imperatives: 'do not judge', 'do not condemn', 'forgive' and 'give'. Each of these imperatives, if acted on, will bring positive consequences of compassionate love. These verses of Luke's gospel, like the Sermon on the Mount, confirm that we are called to imitate the goodness of the Father.

Should we strive for perfection?
For people trapped in situations where there is no compassion or human warmth, we pray.

TUESDAY OF THE SECOND WEEK IN LENT

A reading from the prophet Isaiah (1:10, 16-20)

Hear what the LORD says, you rulers of Sodom!
Listen to the teaching of our God, you people of Gomorrah.
'Wash, make yourselves clean,
take your wrong-doing out of my sight.
Cease doing evil, learn to do good,
search for justice, discipline the violent,
be just to the orphan, plead for the widow.
Come, let us talk this over,' says the LORD.
'Though your sins are like scarlet,

they shall be white as snow;
though they are red as crimson, they shall be like wool.
If you are willing and listen,
you shall eat the good things of the earth.
But if you refuse and rebel,
you shall be devoured by the sword,
for the mouth of the LORD has spoken.'

THE PROPHET BEGINS HIS stern address in this opening chapter of the book of Isaiah by likening the people to the inhabitants of Sodom and Gomorrah (Genesis 18-19), who merited destruction because of their sin. A string of imperatives urges Israel to change. The prophet begins with 'wash', 'make yourselves clean', 'take your wrong-doing out of my sight'. The specific crimes of Israel involve injustice, especially to the orphan and the widow, who are so vulnerable. But change is possible, as from red to white, bringing a new start of holiness, provided that Israel is 'willing' and 'listens'. Israel is free to follow the word of God through the prophet, or to 'refuse' and 'rebel'.

> **Psalm 50 (49)** in a similar fashion accuses Israel of despising the Law of the Lord and disregarding his words. Change, however, is possible.

A reading from the holy gospel according to Matthew (23:1-12)

Then addressing the crowds and his disciples Jesus said, 'The scribes and the Pharisees occupy the chair of Moses. You must therefore do and observe everything that they tell you; but do not do what they do, since they do not practise what they teach. They tie up heavy burdens and lay them on people's shoulders, but they do not lift a finger to move them. Everything they do is done to be seen by others, for they make their headbands broader and their tassels longer. They love the place of honour at banquets and the front seats in the synagogues, and greetings in the market squares and to be addressed by people as Rabbi. 'You, however, must not allow yourselves to be called Rabbi, since you have only one Master, and you are all brothers and sisters. You must call no one on earth your father, since you have only one Father, and he is in heaven. Nor must you allow yourselves to be called teachers, for you have only one Teacher, the Messiah. The greatest among you will be your servant. Anyone who raises himself up will be humbled, and anyone who humbles himself will be raised up.'

IT IS EASY TO concentrate on the supposed faults of others. The first half of this gospel passage points to the behaviour of the scribes and Pharisees, religious experts, who just like those of today are tempted to take pride in their status and importance. They are determined to be seen and to be admired by the people. But the second half of this passage is for all. There is a focus on the one 'Master', the one 'Father' and the one 'Teacher'. There is no place in Christianity for superior pride. Jesus encourages humility and service, for 'the greatest among you will be your servant'. These later words of the gospel passage invite us to change.

Why is status so important for some religious people?
For the grace to see the greatness of humble service, we pray.

WEDNESDAY OF THE SECOND WEEK IN LENT

A reading from the prophet Jeremiah (18:18-20)
They said, 'Come on, let us concoct a plot against Jeremiah, for priests will never be lost for Law, wise men never be lost for advice, prophets never be lost for the word. Come on, let us slander him and pay no attention to anything he says.'
>Pay attention to me, LORD,
>hear what my adversaries are saying.
>Should evil be returned for good?
>Now they have dug a pit for my life.
>Remember how I stood before you and spoke good of them,
>to turn your wrath away from them.

THE 'CONFESSIONS' OF JEREMIAH contain personal outpourings of the prophet, often similar to the psalms of lament. This short passage begins with words of the enemies of the prophet. Are there not enough priests, wise teachers and prophets? We can surely do without this one! In his prayer the prophet turns to the Lord pleading for assistance. His sense of hurt is compounded, for he has spoken only the truth. They have 'dug a pit' for him, though he has constantly interceded for them. Jeremiah 38 reports that the prophet was thrown by his enemies into a muddy cistern.

> **Psalm 31 (30)** has a similar tone to the words of Jeremiah's confession. The psalmist pleads for release from those who slander him, and expresses his trust in the Lord.

A reading from the holy gospel according to Matthew (20:17-28)

Jesus was going up to Jerusalem, and on the road he took the Twelve aside on their own and said to them, 'Look, we are going up to Jerusalem, and the Son of man will be handed over to the chief priests and scribes. They will condemn him to death and will hand him over to the gentiles to be mocked and scourged and crucified; and on the third day he will be raised up again.'

Then the mother of Zebedee's sons came with her sons to make a request of him, and worshipped him; and he said to her, 'What do you want?' She said to him, 'Promise that these two sons of mine may sit one at your right hand and the other at your left in your kingdom.' Jesus answered, 'You do not know what you are asking. Can you drink the cup that I am going to drink?' They replied, 'We can.' He said to them, 'The cup you shall drink, but as for sitting at my right hand and my left, this is not mine to grant; that is for those for whom it has been prepared by my Father.'

When the other ten heard this they were indignant with the two brothers. But Jesus called them to him and said, 'You know that among the gentiles the rulers lord it over them, and great men tyrannise them. Among you this is not to happen. No; anyone who wants to become great among you must be your servant, and anyone who wants to be first among you must be your servant, just as the Son of man came not to be served but to serve, and to give his life as a ransom for many.'

IN ANSWER TO PETER'S question about the reward the disciples could expect, Jesus has already promised they would sit 'on twelve thrones' (19:28). So it is no surprise that the mother of the two sons of Zebedee, James and John, brings them to Jesus to make a request for places of honour in the kingdom. They are zealous for the kingdom, and, when Jesus speaks of the 'cup' of suffering, they remain committed. But places of honour in the kingdom are not the concern of Jesus, for they are 'prepared by the Father'. When the other ten disciples hear about the conversation they are annoyed. Jesus speaks of how the 'gentiles' crave power and position. For the twelve by contrast there is the call to be a 'servant'. Jesus understands himself in this way: he came to serve and 'give his life as a ransom for many'. The suffering servant in Isaiah 53 is the model, for he 'gives his life as a sin offering'.

It takes time for the full implications of discipleship to sink in.
For those who seek power and position for themselves, and not for service, we pray.

THURSDAY OF THE SECOND WEEK IN LENT

A reading from the prophet Jeremiah (17:5-10)
Thus says the LORD,
'Cursed be anyone who trusts in human beings,
who relies on human strength
and whose heart turns away from the LORD.
Such a one is like a shrub in the wastelands,
living in the parched places of the desert,
uninhabited, salt land;
when good comes it brings no benefit!
Blessed is anyone who trusts in the LORD,
with the LORD to rely on.
Such a one is like a tree by the waterside
that thrusts its roots to the stream:
when the heat comes it has nothing to fear,
its foliage stays green;

SECOND WEEK IN LENT

untroubled in a year of drought,
it never stops bearing fruit.
The heart is more devious than any other thing,
it is perverse; who can pierce its secrets?
I, the LORD, search the heart, test the motives,
to give each person what such conduct and such actions deserve.'

THE PROPHET REFLECTS ON the question of trust. In whom do we put our faith: in human beings, or in the Lord? The strong language of 'curse' brings home just how fundamental the question is. Faith in what is human implies turning away from the Lord. This may be in the political context so familiar to Jeremiah, or in the everyday dealings of human life. Such a person is like a weak shrub in a barren wasteland, a waterless, salty wilderness. The contrasting image, for the one who trusts in the Lord, is the tree by the stream, with deep roots reaching the life-giving waters. Even in time of heat or in a year of drought, even in times of political or personal crisis, it still bears green foliage and plentiful fruit. The reading ends with the assertion that God alone reads human hearts and rewards people according to their actions.

> **Psalm 1** inverses the order found in Jeremiah's words, beginning with the one who finds delight in the law of the Lord, again compared to a tree by flowing waters. The wicked, by contrast, are driven away by the wind.

A reading from the holy gospel according to Luke (16:19-31)

Jesus said 'There was a rich man who used to dress in purple and fine linen and feast magnificently every day. And at his gate there used to lie a poor man called Lazarus, covered with sores, who longed to fill himself with what fell from the rich man's table. Even dogs came and licked his sores. Now it happened that the poor man died and was carried away by the angels into Abraham's embrace. The rich man also died and was buried. In his torment in Hades he looked up and saw Abraham a long way off with Lazarus in his embrace. So he cried out, "Father Abraham, have mercy on me and send Lazarus to dip the tip of his finger in water and cool my tongue, for I am in agony in these flames." Abraham said, "My son, remember that during your life you had your fill of good things, just as Lazarus his fill of bad. Now he is being comforted here while you are in agony. But that is not all: between us and you a great gulf has been fixed, to block those who want to cross from our side to yours or from your side to ours." So he said, "Father, I beg you then to send Lazarus to my father's house, since I have five brothers, to give them warning so that they do not come to this place of torment too." Abraham said, "They have Moses and the prophets, let them listen to them." The rich man replied, "Ah no, father Abraham, but if someone comes to them from the dead, they will repent." Then Abraham said to him, "If they will not listen either to Moses or to the prophets, they will not be convinced even if someone should rise from the dead."'

A POWERFUL PARABLE, FOUND only in Luke, illustrates the choice human beings must make between selfishness and generosity, raising the perennial issue of the rich man's disregard for the poor at his gate. The prophets urged people to care for those in need, often accusing them of careless disregard (Amos 6). In this parable Jesus portrays not only the contrasting figures of the rich man and Lazarus, but also Abraham as the arbiter of the case. Jesus emphasises the stubbornness of the rich man, who even after death tries to bully the patriarch Abraham to 'send Lazarus', still regarded as less than a slave, to bring water to cool his tongue. But a 'great gulf' now separates the rich from Lazarus 'in the embrace' of Abraham. It is too late. But the rich man insists that Lazarus be dispatched to warn his five brothers, who, it is implied, are just as bad as he is. They may indeed habitually disregard 'Moses and the prophets', but, the rich man pleads, if someone comes to them from the dead, 'they will repent'. Abraham is not persuaded. There is a sense of inevitability that the five brothers, and countless more like them, will continue through history to disregard the poor man, and whole populations of the poor, at the gate.

What will make us see care for the planet, and care for the poor, as God's priorities, which we must make our own?
For those who strive to change hearts and minds, we pray.

SECOND WEEK IN LENT

FRIDAY OF THE SECOND WEEK IN LENT

A reading from the book of Genesis (37:3-4, 12-13, 17-28)

Israel loved Joseph more than all his other sons, for he was the son of his old age, and he had a coloured tunic made for him. But his brothers, seeing how much more his father loved him than all his other sons, came to hate him so much that they could not say a peaceful word to him.

His brothers went to pasture their father's flock at Shechem. Then Israel said to Joseph, 'Your brothers are looking after the flock at Shechem, aren't they? Come, I am going to send you to them.' So Joseph went after his brothers and found them at Dothan.

They saw him from a distance, and before he reached them they made a plot to kill him. They said to one another, 'Here comes that dreamer. Come on, let us kill him now and throw him down one of the pits; we can say that some wild animal has devoured him. Then we shall see what becomes of his dreams.'

But Reuben heard, and he saved him from their hands; he said, 'Let us not take his life.' Reuben said to them, 'Do not shed blood; throw him into that pit out in the desert, but do not lay hands on him' – wanting to save him from their hands and to restore him to his father. So, when Joseph reached his brothers, they pulled off his tunic, the coloured tunic that he was wearing, and catching hold of him, threw him into the pit. The pit was empty, with no water in it. They then sat down to eat.

Looking up, they saw a group of Ishmaelites coming from Gilead, their camels laden with gum, balsam and resin, which they were taking to Egypt. Then Judah said to his brothers, 'What do we gain by killing our brother and hiding his blood? Come, let us sell him to the Ishmaelites, then we shall not have laid hands on him ourselves. After all, he is our brother, and our own flesh.' His brothers agreed.

Now some Midianite merchants were passing, and they pulled Joseph out of the well. They sold Joseph to the Ishmaelites for twenty shekels of silver, and these took Joseph to Egypt.

IN THIS READING WE hear the opening stages of the story of Joseph from the book of Genesis, a story that covers several chapters. As this gripping short story unfolds, Joseph, despite being sold as a slave, will be raised to power in Egypt and be able to assist his brothers who descend into Egypt due to the famine in their own land. Once he has revealed his identity to his brothers, Joseph himself will proclaim that God turned the evil they did to him into good, sending him before them to be able to save their lives (Genesis 45). Once again, as in the case of the prophet Jeremiah, a figure from the Hebrew Scriptures stands as a preparation for Jesus: Joseph becomes saviour of his people. The passage also illustrates the frequent failure of flawed human persons: the father Jacob who displays preferential love for Joseph (just as Jacob's mother Rebekah had done in his favour), and thereby provokes jealousy and hatred among brothers.

> **Psalm 105 (104)** is a historical psalm which covers the descent into Egypt and the exodus. A few verses recall the story of Joseph sold as a slave and then released and given power.

A reading from the holy gospel according to Matthew (21:33-43, 45-46)

Jesus said: 'Listen to another parable. There was a man, a landowner, who planted a vineyard; he fenced it round, dug a winepress in it and built a tower; then he leased it to tenants and went abroad. When vintage time drew near he sent his servants to the tenants to collect his produce. But the tenants seized his servants, thrashed one, killed another and stoned a third. Next he sent some more servants, this time a larger number, and they dealt with them in the same way. Finally he sent his son to them, thinking, "They will respect my son." But when the tenants saw the son, they said among themselves, "This is the heir. Come on, let us kill him and get his inheritance." So they seized him and threw him out of the vineyard and killed him. Now when the owner of the vineyard comes, what will he do to those tenants?' They answered, 'He will bring those wretches to a wretched end and lease the vineyard to other tenants who will deliver the produce to him at the proper time.' Jesus said to them, 'Have you never read in the scriptures:

*The stone which the builders rejected
has become the cornerstone;
this is the Lord's doing
and it is amazing in our eyes?*

'I tell you, then, that the kingdom of God will be taken from you and given to a people who will produce its fruit.'

When they heard his parables, the chief priests and the Pharisees realised he was speaking about them, but though they would have liked to arrest him they were afraid of the crowds, who looked on him as a prophet.

JESUS FACES HOSTILITY FROM the religious leaders in Jerusalem. They have been poor tenants, reacting with violence to those sent to collect the fruits of the Lord's vineyard. The owner of the vineyard has even sent his son, who is killed by the tenants. As a result the kingdom of God will be taken away from them and given to a new people, who will produce appropriate fruit. The rejection of the prophets and of the Son will lead to a new dispensation open to people of other lands. Jesus uses a verse from Psalm 112 which speaks of a rejected stone becoming a cornerstone: 'the stone which the builders rejected has become the cornerstone'. This parable is a severe indictment of the religious leaders, which surely added to the danger facing Jesus in Jerusalem. And yet the 'crowds' were more wise, and knew him to be a prophet of God.

Reflect on how God uses negative situations to create new openings of grace.
For all who are stuck in their own incomplete righteousness, we pray.

SATURDAY OF THE SECOND WEEK IN LENT

A reading from the prophet Micah (7:14-15, 18-20)
With a shepherd's crook lead your people to pasture,
the flock that is your heritage,
living alone in a forest, in the midst of a garden land.

Let them graze in Bashan and Gilead as in the days of old!
Let us see wonders,
as in the days when you came out of the land of Egypt!
What god can compare with you
for pardoning guilt and for overlooking crime
for the remnant of his heritage?
He does not harbour anger for ever
since he delights in faithful love.
Return and have mercy on us,
tread down our faults;
throw all our sins to the bottom of the sea.
Grant Jacob your faithfulness
and Abraham your faithful love,
as you swore to our ancestors
from the days of long ago.

THESE WORDS FROM THE end of the book of Micah focus on the mercy of God, which will be richly illustrated in the gospel. God who cares for the people is often portrayed as shepherd (Psalm 80). The people are to 'graze', as in Bashan and Gilead, fertile land taken over during the conquest of the land. But God is called upon to do new 'wonders', such as were worked when they came out of Egypt. God 'delights in faithful love' (*hesed*). God will show mercy and submerge all memory of sin to the bottom of the sea, another allusion to the exodus, when Pharaoh's armies were drowned. Now it is the greater enemy, sin, which is destroyed. In this way God maintains the faithfulness promised long ago to the patriarchs and renews it.

> **Psalm 103 (102)** This great psalm of forgiveness reflects the words of Micah. The Lord is compassion and love, slow to anger, rich in mercy, removing sins 'as far as the east is from the west'.

A reading from the holy gospel according to Luke (15:1-3, 11-32)

The tax collectors and sinners, however, were all crowding round to listen to him, and the Pharisees and scribes complained saying, 'This man welcomes sinners and eats with them.' So he told them this parable.

'There was a man who had two sons. The younger one said to his father, "Father, let me have the share of the estate that will come to me." So the father divided the property between them. A few days later, the younger son got together everything he had and left for a distant country where he squandered his money in loose living.

'When he had spent it all, that country experienced a severe famine, and now he began to be in need; so he hired himself out to one of the local inhabitants who sent him into the fields to feed the pigs. And he would willingly have filled himself with the pods which the pigs were eating, but no one would let him have them. Then he came to his senses and said, "How many of my father's hired men have all the food they want and more, and here am I dying of hunger! I will get up and go to my father and say: Father, I have sinned against heaven and against you; I no longer deserve to be called your son; treat me as one of your hired men." So he got up and went back to his father.

'While he was still a long way off, his father saw him and was moved with pity. He ran to the boy, clasped him in his arms and kissed him. Then his son said, "Father, I have sinned against heaven and against you. I no longer deserve to be called your son." But the father said to his servants, "Quick! Bring out the best robe and put it on him; put a ring on his finger and sandals on his feet. Bring the fattened calf, and kill it; we will celebrate by having a feast, because this son of mine was dead and has come back to life; he was lost and is found." And they began to celebrate.

'Now the elder son was out in the fields, and on his way back, as he drew near the house, he heard music and dancing. Calling one of the servants he asked what it was all about. The servant told him, "Your brother has come, and your father has killed the fattened calf because he has got him back safe and sound." He was angry then and refused to go in, and his father came out and began to plead with him; but he retorted to his father, "Look! All these years I have slaved for you and never disobeyed your orders, yet you never gave me so much as a young goat for me to celebrate with my friends. But, for this son of yours, when he comes back after swallowing up your property with prostitutes you kill the fattened calf."

Then the father said, "My son, you are with me always and all I have is yours. But it was only right we should celebrate and rejoice, because your brother here was dead and has come to life; he was lost and is found."'

THE PARABLE OF THE son who was lost and is found, the prodigal who comes back to life, can best be understood from the opening words of the chapter, that the Pharisees and scribes 'complained' that Jesus associated with sinners. Unique to Luke's gospel, this parable contrasts the wild behaviour of the younger son with the dutiful service of his elder brother. The younger son who has the humility to seek forgiveness is welcomed back with a new robe, with music and feasting. It is the older son who has the greater problem. Is it possible for him to open his heart in forgiveness to his brother, whom he angrily dismisses while speaking to his father as 'this son of yours'? The older boy stands for the religious leaders who are shocked by the mercy shown by Jesus. This 'scandal' of forgiveness is a constant in Christian history. That the lost should be found, and that the dead should be raised, these hopes, these realities, lie at the heart of the gospel. Recognising one's own need for mercy may well be the key to accepting with gratitude the mercy God shows to others.

Why is it so difficult to accept God's tender mercy shown to others? For those who see mercy as soft and as a violation of God's justice, we pray.

Third Week in Lent

THIRD SUNDAY OF LENT – YEAR A

A reading from the book of Exodus (17:3-7)
In their thirst for water the people complained to Moses, saying, 'Why did you bring us up out of Egypt, only to make us, our children and our livestock, die of thirst?' Moses cried out to the LORD, saying, 'What am I to do with this people? They are almost ready to stone me!'

Then the LORD said to Moses, 'Go on ahead of the people, taking some of the elders of Israel with you; in your hand take the staff with which you struck the river, and go. I shall be waiting for you there on the rock at Horeb. Strike the rock, and water will come out for the people to drink.' Moses did so, with the elders of Israel watching. He gave the place the names Massah and Meribah because the Israelites had quarrelled and put the LORD to the test by saying, 'Is the LORD among us, or not?'

AT THIS POINT IN the book of Exodus the people have crossed the sea and are travelling through the desert towards Sinai (Horeb). The privations of desert life lead them to regret coming out of Egypt. God has provided food for them in the form of the manna and the quails (Exodus 16). Moses is now blamed for the lack of water, and he fears for his life. The place where water sprang from the rock is given the names Massah and Meribah, Hebrew terms which mean 'trial' and 'contention'. This theme will occur again later in the story of the wandering in the desert after the stay at Sinai (Numbers 20). Life-giving water is the theme in each of the readings today.

> **Psalm 95 (94)** also refers to the incident of Massah and Meribah, and proclaims God as the 'rock of salvation'.

A reading from the letter of St Paul to the Romans (5:1-2, 5-8)

So, now that we have been justified by faith, we have peace with God through our Lord Jesus Christ; it is through him, by faith, that we have received access to the favour of God in which we are living, and we exult in the hope of the glory of God. Hope does not disappoint, since the love of God has been poured into our hearts by the Holy Spirit given to us. When we were still helpless, at the due time, Christ died for the godless. Scarcely will anyone die for a righteous person, though for a good person perhaps someone might undertake to die. So God proves his love for us, that while we were still sinners Christ died for us.

ST PAUL RESTATES THE situation of the faithful Christian, justified by faith in Jesus Christ, and at peace with God. Furthermore, 'the hope of the glory of God' is bestowed on the Christian, since the love of God 'has been poured into our hearts by the Holy Spirit'. It is no surprise that this love is said to have been 'poured' like water: water is essentially life-giving, and baptism is being recalled. The gifts of God in Christ came to us despite human sinfulness. Christians are the recipients of God's gift of the Holy Spirit at baptism, and throughout their lives.

A reading from the holy gospel according to John (4:5-42)

So Jesus came to the Samaritan town called Sychar, near the land that Jacob had given to his son Joseph. Jacob's well was there and Jesus, tired by the journey, was sitting by the well. It was about noon, when a Samaritan woman came to draw water. Jesus said to her, 'Give me a drink.' His disciples had gone into the town to buy food. The Samaritan said to him, 'How is it that you, a Jew, ask me, a Samaritan woman, for a drink?' – for Jews do not associate with Samaritans. Jesus replied to her:

'If you knew what God is offering
and who it is saying to you, "Give me a drink",
you would have asked him,
and he would have given you living water.'

She answered, 'Sir, you have no bucket, and the well is deep. Where do you get this living water? Are you a greater man than our father

Jacob, who gave us this well and drank from it, himself and his sons and his cattle?' Jesus replied:

'Whoever drinks of this water
will be thirsty again;
but anyone who drinks of the water that I shall give
will never be thirsty again:
the water that I shall give
will become an inner spring of water, welling up to eternal life.'

The woman said to him, 'Sir, give me this water, so that I may never be thirsty or go on coming here to draw water.' Jesus said to her, 'Go and call your husband and come back here.' The woman answered him saying, 'I have no husband.' Jesus said to her, 'You are right to say, "I have no husband"; for you have had five men, and the one you now have is not your husband. You spoke the truth there.' The woman said to him, 'Sir, I see you are a prophet. Our fathers worshipped on this mountain, though you say that the place where people should worship is in Jerusalem.' Jesus said:

'Believe me, woman, the hour is coming
when you will worship the Father
neither on this mountain nor in Jerusalem.
You worship what you do not know;
we worship what we do know;
for salvation is from the Jews.
But the hour is coming – and is now here –
when true worshippers will worship the Father in spirit and truth,
for such are the worshippers
whom the Father seeks.
God is spirit,
and those who worship him
must worship in spirit and truth.'

The woman said to him, 'I know that Messiah, the one called Christ, is coming; and when he comes he will declare everything.' Jesus said, 'I am he, the one who is speaking to you.'

At this point his disciples returned and were surprised to find him speaking to a woman, but none of them asked, 'What do you want?' or, 'Why are you talking to her?'

The woman left her water jar and went off to the town and said to the people, 'Come and see a man who has told me everything I have ever done. Could this be the Messiah?' They came out of the town and they made their way towards him.

Meanwhile, the disciples were urging him, 'Rabbi, have something to eat'; but he said, 'I have food to eat that you do not know about.' So the disciples said to one another, 'Has someone brought him food?' But Jesus said:

'My food is to do the will of the one who sent me,
and to complete his work.
Do you not say,
"Four months and then the harvest"?
Well, I tell you,
look around you, look at the fields;
they are white for the harvest!
Already the reaper is being paid his wages,
already he is bringing in the grain for eternal life,
so that sower and reaper may rejoice together.
For here the proverb holds true:
one sows, another reaps;
I sent you to reap
a harvest for which you did not labour.
Others have laboured;
and you have come into the rewards of their labour.'

Many Samaritans of that town believed in him on the strength of the words of the woman's witness, 'He told me everything I have done.' So, when the Samaritans came to him, they asked him to stay with them. He stayed there for two days, and many more came to believe on the strength of the words he spoke to them; and they said to the woman, 'We believe no longer because of what you told us; we have heard for ourselves and we know that this is truly the Saviour of the world.'

THREE GREAT JOHANNINE GOSPELS punctuate the road to Easter. They feature: the woman of Samaria (John 4); the man born blind (John 9); and the raising of Lazarus (John 11). The theme today is 'living water', the topic of conversation between Jesus and the woman of Samaria. Jesus arrives, tired and thirsty in the middle of the day, and sits by the well, the well of Jacob. The woman is unnamed, she has a chequered history, but she is ready to learn. After a discussion about 'living water', the question of the identity of Jesus arises. He is surely a prophet, or perhaps even the Messiah. Jesus declares: 'I am he.' This concludes the dialogue, for the woman, having discovered one who can give 'living water', leaves her empty water jar, and rushes off to call the villagers. This missionary disciple, the despised woman befriended by Jesus, brings them to faith, and that faith is confirmed by hearing the message from the lips of Jesus himself. They know that 'this is truly the Saviour of the world'.

How is the journey of faith of the Samaritan woman like your own? Pray that on our journey we may be open to the surprises of God.

THIRD SUNDAY OF LENT – YEAR B

A reading from the book of Exodus (20:1-17)

Then God spoke all these words. He said, 'I am the LORD your God who brought you out of the land of Egypt, out of the house of slavery.

'You shall have no other gods before me.

'You shall not make yourself a carved image or any likeness of anything in heaven above or on earth beneath or in the waters under the earth.

'You shall not bow down to them or serve them. For I, the LORD your God, am a jealous God and I punish a parent's fault in the children, to the third and fourth generation of those who hate me; but I act with faithful love towards thousands of those who love me and keep my commandments.

'You shall not misuse the name of the LORD your God, for the LORD will not acquit anyone who misuses his name.

'Remember the Sabbath day and keep it holy. For six days you shall labour and do all your work, but the seventh day is a Sabbath for the LORD your God. You shall do no work that day, neither you nor your son nor your daughter nor your slaves, men or women, nor your animals nor the foreigner living with you. For in six days the LORD made the heavens, earth and sea and all that these contain, but on the seventh day he rested; that is why the LORD has blessed the Sabbath day and made it sacred.

'Honour your father and your mother so that you may live long in the land that the LORD your God is giving you.

'You shall not murder.

'You shall not commit adultery.

'You shall not steal.

'You shall not give false evidence against your neighbour.

'You shall not covet your neighbour's house. You shall not covet your neighbour's spouse, or slave, man or woman, or ox, or donkey, or anything that belongs to your neighbour.'

AFTER LEAVING EGYPT THE Israelites travel to the holy mountain, known both as Sinai and Horeb, where they meet God (Exodus 19). This is the place of the covenant between God and the people. The 'ten words' which follow spell out the covenant obligation of Israel. It is God who has brought Israel out of slavery, and who lays down rules for them to live in freedom. There is to be no acknowledgement of other gods. Idolatry is the first and most serious transgression. God is 'jealous', for it is this God alone who is real, and who loves and cares for people. Punishment is announced for sins, 'to the third and fourth generation' of those who 'hate me', but there is no limit to God's 'kindness', his covenant love (*hesed*), towards the thousands who 'love me' and who keep the commandments. The commandments list solemn duties towards God, such as the sabbath, and towards brothers and sisters. They are a basis on which both Judaism and Christianity will build.

> **Psalm 19 (18)** This psalm and its longer counterpart in Psalm 119 rejoice in the Law. It is given for our delight and to assist our freedom; it is more desirable than gold, and 'sweeter than honey flowing from the comb'.

A reading from the first letter of St Paul to the Corinthians (1:22-25)

While the Jews demand signs and the Greeks seek wisdom, we are proclaiming a crucified Christ: to the Jews a stumbling-block, to the gentiles foolishness, but to those who have been called, both Jews and

Greeks, a Christ who is both the power of God and the wisdom of God. God's folly is wiser than human wisdom, and God's weakness is stronger than human strength.

PAUL, WITH HIS COSMOPOLITAN background, is keenly aware of what Jews and Greeks seek. Neither is satisfied, it seems, with what God offers. The Jews look for signs, and are scandalised by the gospel of death and resurrection. The gentiles search for wisdom, and find foolishness. For the Jews the crucifixion of the Messiah is a 'stumbling-block' (*skandalon*), never anticipated in their scriptures. For Greeks it is sheer madness (*moria*). God brings human beings to realise by grace that in the cross of Christ lie both the power and wisdom of God, for death is overcome in resurrection.

A reading from the holy gospel according to John (2:13-25)

The time of the Jewish Passover was near and Jesus went up to Jerusalem. In the Temple he found people selling cattle and sheep and doves, and the money-changers sitting there. Making a whip out of cords, he began to drive them all out of the Temple, both sheep and cattle, scattered the money-changers' coins, overturned their tables and said to the dove-sellers, 'Take all this away from here and stop making my Father's house a market-house.' Then his disciples remembered that it had been written, *I am eaten up with zeal for your house.* The Jews in reply said, 'What sign can you show us for doing this?' Jesus answered, 'Destroy this Temple, and in three days I will raise it up.' The Jews replied, 'It took forty-six years to build this Temple: are you going to raise it up in three days?' But he was speaking about the Temple that was his body. When he had been raised from the dead, his disciples remembered that he had said this, and they believed the scripture and the words that he had spoken.

While he was in Jerusalem for the festival of the Passover many believed in his name because they saw the signs that he did, but Jesus did not trust himself to them, since he knew all people. He needed no witness about anyone; he himself knew what was in everyone.

THE ACTION OF JESUS in the temple is provocative. He defends the holiness of the Father's house, where the court of the Gentiles has been taken over for the sale of sacrificial animals and the exchange of currency. The ensuing conversation goes deeper and Jesus offers as justification the 'sign' of his own resurrection, a sign misunderstood by his opponents and understood only later by the disciples. He is the sign of a new reality, of resurrection to new life. We should notice the concluding statements of the evangelist, that 'many believed in his name because they saw the signs that he did'. The signs of John's gospel present the paschal mystery of death and resurrection in multiple ways, and many will come to faith.

What are the unexpected signs which point to faith?
Pray for an understanding that everything is connected and laid before us by the love of God.

THIRD SUNDAY OF LENT – YEAR C

A reading from the book of Exodus (3:1-8, 13-15)

Moses was looking after the flock of his father-in-law Jethro, the priest of Midian; he led it to the far side of the desert and came to Horeb, the mountain of God. The angel of the LORD appeared to him in a flame blazing from the middle of a bush. Moses looked; there was the bush blazing, but the bush was not being burnt up. Moses said, 'I must go over and see this strange sight, and why the bush is not being burnt up.' When the LORD saw him going over to look, God called to him from the middle of the bush, saying, 'Moses, Moses!' He answered, 'Here I am!' Then he said, 'Come no nearer! Remove the sandals from your feet, for the place where you are standing is holy ground.' And he said, 'I am the God of your ancestors, the God of Abraham, the God of Isaac and the God of Jacob.' At this Moses covered his face, for he was afraid to look at God.

Then the LORD said, 'I have indeed seen the misery of my people in Egypt. I have heard them crying for help because of their taskmasters. I know their sufferings, and I have come down to rescue them from the hands of the Egyptians and bring them up out of that land, to a land rich and broad, a land flowing with milk and honey.

Moses then said to God, 'Look, if I go to the Israelites and say to them, "The God of your ancestors has sent me to you," and they say to me, "What is his name?", what shall I say to them?' God said to Moses, 'I am who I am.' And he said, 'This is what you are to say to the Israelites, "I am has sent me to you."' God further said to Moses, 'You are to tell the Israelites, "The LORD, the God of your ancestors, the God of Abraham, the God of Isaac and the God of Jacob, has sent me to you." This is my name for all time, and this is my title for all generations.

THIS NARRATIVE HAS ENORMOUS significance. It is our first glimpse of the holy mountain, known both as Sinai and Horeb. Moses, who has been tending the flocks of Jethro, finds himself in a life-changing encounter with a holy God. And yet this apparently inaccessible God is the God of named ancestors, a God who has become involved in the past and will be involved in a very significant way now. For God knows the pain and suffering of the people of Israel in Egypt. Deliverance from slavery is promised and we hear for the first time in Scripture the phrase 'land of milk and honey'. An equally significant feature of this reading is the revelation of the 'name' of God, in the mysterious formula 'I Am who I Am' (*'ehyeh 'asher 'ehyeh*). This is the God who 'is' but who also 'is' for people. The name given to Moses is so sacred that it is never pronounced either in Jewish or Christian tradition.

> **Psalm 103 (102)** That the Lord is 'compassionate and generous' suggests that God will indeed intervene in the rescue of his people.

A reading from the first letter of St Paul to the Corinthians (10:1-6, 10-12)

I want you to be quite clear, brothers and sisters, that our ancestors were all under the cloud and all passed through the sea. And all were baptised into Moses in the cloud and in the sea. All ate the same spiritual food, and all drank the same spiritual drink, since they drank from the spiritual rock which followed them, and the rock was Christ. Nevertheless, God was not pleased with most of them, and their corpses were scattered over the desert. Now these things happened as examples, so that we should never set our hearts on evil things, as they did. Do not complain, as some of them complained and they were destroyed by the Destroyer.

Now all these things happened to them by way of example, and they were written down to instruct us on whom the ends of the ages have come. So anyone who thinks to be standing firm should take care not to fall.

THE CORINTHIAN CHRISTIANS MUST take a warning from the journey of Israel in the desert. Paul links the cloud and the sea to Baptism, and the food and living water from the rock he considers gifts of the pre-existent Christ. Despite such gifts the Israelites did not please God and perished in the desert (Numbers 14). Paul now gives a stern warning to the Christians of Corinth, who have been baptised and are nourished in the Eucharist, to be especially careful, since 'the ends of the ages' are near. They should be careful not to fall.

A reading from the holy gospel according to Luke (13:1-9)

On this occasion some people were present who told him about the Galileans whose blood Pilate had mingled with that of their sacrifices. In reply he said to them, 'Do you suppose that these Galileans were worse sinners than all other Galileans, that this should have happened to them? No, I tell you, but unless you repent you will all perish as they did. Or those eighteen on whom the tower at Siloam fell, killing them? Do you suppose that they were more guilty than all the other people living in Jerusalem? No; but unless you repent you will all perish as they did.'

He told this parable, 'A man had a fig tree planted in his vineyard, and he came looking for fruit on it but found none. He said to the gardener, "For three years now I have been coming to look for fruit on this fig tree and finding none. Cut it down: why should it be taking up the ground?" In reply he said, "Sir, leave it just this year and give me time to dig round it and manure it: it may bear fruit next year; if not, then you can cut it down."'

THIS UNIQUE TEACHING OF Jesus raises profound problems. Jesus recounts two examples of undeserved suffering, one caused by human cruelty and the other by an accident. It is not appropriate to consider as guilty those who are victims of innocent suffering. Jesus is implicitly recalling the teaching of the book of Job. Yet he repeats the call to repentance, which is always pressing. The parable, in contrast, is an enchanting reminder of God's mercy. The gardener does not hesitate to ask for one more year, trusting in the leniency of the owner of the garden. Yet the conversation ends without revealing this man's reply. Is this an assurance of mercy, or a stern warning of the urgency of repentance?

How can God be holy and remote, and at the same time involved with people?
Pray for a balance between presuming on God's mercy and urgent repentance.

MONDAY OF THE THIRD WEEK IN LENT

A reading from the second book of Kings (5:1-15)

Naaman, army commander to the king of Aram, was a man who enjoyed his master's respect and favour, since through him the LORD had granted victory to the Aramaeans. But the man suffered from leprosy. Now, on one of their raids into Israelite territory, the Aramaeans had carried off a little girl, who became a servant of Naaman's wife. She said to her mistress, 'If only my master would approach the prophet of Samaria! He would cure him of his leprosy.' Naaman went and told his master, saying, 'This and this is what the girl from Israel said.' The king of Aram said, 'Go by all means. I shall send a letter to the king of Israel.' So Naaman left, taking with him ten talents of silver, six thousand shekels of gold and ten festal robes. He brought the letter to the king of Israel. It read, 'When this letter reaches you, I am sending my servant Naaman to you for you to cure him of his leprosy.' When the king of Israel read the letter, he tore his clothes. He said, 'Am I a god to give death and life, for him to send a man to me and ask me to cure him of his leprosy? Just look and see how he means to pick a quarrel with me.'

When Elisha heard that the king of Israel had torn his clothes, he sent word to the king, 'Why have you torn your clothes? Let him come to me, and he will learn that there is a prophet in Israel.' So Naaman came with his team and chariot and drew up at the door of

Elisha's house. And Elisha sent a messenger to him, saying, 'Go and bathe seven times in the Jordan, and your flesh will become clean.' But Naaman was indignant and went off, saying, 'Here was I, thinking that for me he would be sure to come out, and stand there, and call on the name of the LORD his God, and wave his hand over the spot and cure the part that was diseased. Surely, Abana and Parpar, the rivers of Damascus, are better than any water in Israel? Could I not bathe in them to become clean?' And he turned round and went off in a fury. But his servants approached him and spoke to him, saying, 'Father, if the prophet had asked you to do something difficult, would you not have done it? All the more reason, then, when he says to you, "Wash and become clean."' So he went down and immersed himself seven times in the Jordan, as the man of God had told him to do. And his flesh became clean once more like the flesh of a little child.

Returning to the man of God with his whole escort, he went in and, presenting himself, said, 'Now I know that there is no God anywhere on earth except in Israel.

NAAMAN IS AN OUTSIDER, and for two reasons. Why should an Aramean be healed by a prophet of Israel? Furthermore, he suffers from leprosy. It is the voice of the Israelite servant girl that speaks the truth and opens the way to the working of God's mercy through the prophet Elisha. Naaman, like the king of Israel before him, is at first indignant at having to bathe in the river Jordan seven times. Once again wisdom comes from the servants, who counsel him to do what the prophet asks. Naaman, who has humbled himself, receives both healing and faith.

> **Psalm 42 (41)** Once again the Lord uses water for life and healing.

A reading from the holy gospel according to Luke (4:24-30)

Jesus said, 'Amen I say to you, no prophet is ever accepted in his own country. In truth I tell you, there were many widows in Israel in Elijah's day, when heaven remained shut for three years and six months and a great famine raged throughout the land, but Elijah was not sent to any one of these, but only *to a widow at Zarephath, a town in Sidonia.* And there were many lepers in Israel in the prophet Elisha's time, but none of these was cured – only Naaman the Syrian.'

When they heard this everyone in the synagogue was enraged. They sprang to their feet and hustled him out of the town; and they took him up to the brow of the hill on which their town was built, intending to throw him off the cliff, but he passed through the midst of them and walked away.

THESE ARE THE FINAL verses of the story of the visit to Nazareth which Luke places at the beginning of the ministry of Jesus. In the synagogue Jesus has proclaimed a reading from the prophet Isaiah and identified himself as the one who has been sent to 'bring good news to the poor'. After initial appreciation the mood changes as Jesus quotes a popular proverb about the rejection of prophets by their own people: 'no prophet is ever accepted in his own country'. They are enraged when he reminds them that Elijah and Elisha worked miracles beyond the confines of Israel: the widow of Zarephath and her son were fed, and Naaman the Syrian restored to full health. Rage leads to violence against Jesus. The people of Nazareth consider that their honoured place as chosen people has been usurped. The message of the kingdom however cannot be confined to a 'chosen' people.

As Christians do we value those of other faiths?
Pray for a heart open to the needs of all, and especially those on the furthest margins.

TUESDAY OF THE THIRD WEEK IN LENT

A reading from the prophet Daniel (3:25, 34-43)

Azariah stood still in the heart of the fire, praying aloud, and he said:
'For the sake of your name do not abandon us for ever,
do not repudiate your covenant,
do not withdraw your mercy
for the sake of Abraham, your friend,

of Isaac, your servant, and of Israel, your holy one,
to whom you promised to make their descendants as many as the stars of heaven
and as the grains of sand on the seashore.
Lord, we have become the least of all nations,
we are put to shame today throughout the world because of our sins.
We now have no leader, no prophet, no prince,
no burnt offering, no sacrifice, no oblation, no incense,
no place where we can make offerings to you and win your mercy.
But in contrition of heart and humility of spirit
may we be as acceptable to you as burnt offerings of rams and bullocks,
as thousands of fat lambs:
such let our sacrifice be to you today
and may it please you that we follow you wholeheartedly
since there is no shame for those who trust in you.
And now with our whole heart we follow you,
we revere you and seek your face once more.
Do not put us to shame
but treat us according to your graciousness,
according to the abundance of your mercy.
Rescue us in accordance with your wonderful deeds
and win fresh glory for your name, O Lord.'

THE EDITOR OF THE book of Daniel has added wonderful prayers to the story of the three young men thrown into the furnace by king Nebuchadnezzar. Azariah's prayer of penance reminds God of the covenant made with Abraham, Isaac and Jacob, as well as acknowledging the sin of the people which has led to their present situation of exile and distress. Azariah provides a list of the things of which they are deprived in their exile in a pagan land, from true leadership to the incense of prayer. Despite this he knows that 'contrition of heart and humility of spirit' are a worthy offering to God, as acceptable as the sacrifices laid down by the law. He asks God to show kindness, 'according to the abundance of your mercy'. In this way God will 'win fresh glory for your name'.

THIRD WEEK IN LENT

> **Psalm 25 (24)** May God 'remember' his compassion and his acts of mercy shown from ancient times, so that God's mercy may be seen again.

A reading from the holy gospel according to Matthew (18:21-35)

Then Peter went up to him and said, 'Lord, how often must I forgive my brother or sister who wrongs me? As often as seven times?' Jesus answered, 'Not seven, I tell you, but seventy-seven times. And so the kingdom of Heaven may be compared to a king who decided to settle accounts with his servants. When he began the reckoning, someone was brought who owed him ten thousand talents; he had no means of paying, so his master gave orders that he should be sold, together with his wife and children and all his possessions, and payment made. So the servant threw himself down at his master's feet, with the words, "Be patient with me and I will pay you everything." And the servant's master felt so sorry for him that he let him go and cancelled the debt. Now on his way out the servant met one of his fellow-servants who owed him one hundred denarii; and he seized him and began to throttle him, saying, "Pay what you owe." His fellow-servant fell at his feet and appealed to him, saying, "Be patient with me and I will pay you." But the other would not agree; on the contrary, he threw him into prison till he should pay the debt. His fellow-servants were deeply distressed at what was happening, and they went and reported to their master everything that had happened. Then the master sent for the man and said to him, "You wicked servant, I cancelled all that debt of yours when you appealed to me. Were you not bound, then, to have pity on your fellow-servant just as I had pity on you?" And in his anger the master handed him over to the torturers till he should pay all his debt. And that is how my heavenly Father will deal with you unless you each forgive your brother and sister from your heart.'

THIS FAMOUS PARABLE OF the unforgiving debtor comes at the end of the discourse on community, the fourth major speech of Jesus in the gospel of Matthew. It is as if the final and most important teaching that communities must learn is about forgiveness, that we should forgive others as we are forgiven by the Lord. The amount of money he owes to the king is astronomical, but the prayer of this first debtor for forgiveness has the effect of his debt being wiped out. The second debtor, who owes comparatively little, a sum a labourer might earn in a matter of weeks, uses the same words in his prayer: 'Be patient with me and I will pay you.' But he fails to obtain forgiveness. The outrageous behaviour of the unforgiving debtor seems almost to justify his terrible punishment.

'Forgive us our sins as we forgive those who sin against us.'
Pray for those who are stuck in resentment and cannot forgive.

WEDNESDAY OF THE THIRD WEEK IN LENT

A reading from the book of Deuteronomy (4:1,5-9)

Moses said to the people: 'And now, Israel, listen to the laws and customs that I am teaching you, so that, by observing them, you may survive to enter and take possession of the land which the LORD, God of your ancestors, is giving you. Look, as the LORD my God commanded me, I am teaching you laws and customs, for you to observe in the country of which you are going to take possession. Keep them, put them into practice, and this will show your wisdom and prudence to other peoples when they hear all these laws; they will exclaim, "No other people is as wise and prudent as this great nation!" And indeed, what great nation has its gods as near as the LORD our God is to us whenever we call to him? And what great nation has laws and customs as righteous as all this Law which I am laying down for you today? But take care, and watch yourselves! Do not forget the things which you yourselves have seen, or let them slip from your heart as long as you live; teach them, rather, to your children and to your children's children.'

THE BOOK OF DEUTERONOMY looks back on the giving of the Law and in a series of speeches attributed to Moses encourages fidelity. Moses is known in Jewish tradition as 'our rabbi' and 'our teacher'. In this reading his role is summarised. Adherence to the Law brings life, and wisdom, so that neighbouring nations will stand in admiration. Israel is also warned of the danger of forgetting what they were taught and ceasing to heed the Law. It is the duty of the Israelite to continue to teach: 'teach them to your children and to your children's children'. Remembrance of things past ensures a better future.

> **Psalm 147** The Lord 'sends out his word to the earth' and 'reveals his word to Jacob'. As in the reading it is stressed that he has not taught other nations.

A reading from the holy gospel according to Matthew (5:17-19)

Jesus said to his disciples: 'Do not think that I have come to abolish the Law or the Prophets. I have come not to abolish but to complete. Amen I say to you, till heaven and earth pass away, not one dot, not one little stroke, will pass from the Law until everything is achieved. Therefore, anyone who infringes even one of the least of these commandments and teaches others to do the same will be called least in the kingdom of Heaven; but anyone who keeps them and teaches them will be called great in the kingdom of Heaven.

THESE IMPORTANT WORDS OF Jesus from the Sermon on the Mount emphasise the continuity between Law and gospel. Jesus brings the Law and the Prophets to fulfilment. These words serve as a prelude to the 'antitheses' (5:21-48), in which Jesus invites a deeper kind of justice. Those who keep and teach the fullness of the Law will be 'called great' in the kingdom. The Law was given to Israel by the love of God; it is proclaimed to Christians as a law of love.

What can I do to bring the Law and the Prophets to fulfilment?
Pray for the Jewish people that they will continue in fidelity to God's covenant.

THURSDAY OF THE THIRD WEEK IN LENT

A reading from the prophet Jeremiah (7:23-28)

The Lord Sabaoth, the God of Israel, says this: 'My one command to them was this: Listen to my voice, then I will be your God and you shall be my people. In everything, follow the way that I mark out for you and you shall prosper. But they did not listen, they did not pay attention; they followed their own devices, their own stubborn and wicked inclinations, and got worse rather than better. From the day your ancestors left the land of Egypt until today, I have sent you all my servants the prophets, persistently sending them day after day. But they have not listened to me, have not paid attention; they have deliberately resisted, behaving worse than their ancestors. So you will tell them all this but they will not listen to you; you will call them but they will not answer you. Then you are to say to them: This is the nation that will neither listen to the voice of the LORD its God nor take correction. Sincerity is no more, it has vanished from their mouths.'

THE JEWISH PRAYER KNOWN as the *shema*, with its opening words 'Listen, Israel,' is recited twice every day. The word 'listen' is found five times in this passage of Jeremiah, either as a command, or in the sorrowful statement 'they did not listen'. Ever since they left Egypt they have disregarded the voice of God's prophets. The history of this people is a history of not listening, and their behaviour has worsened as the generations have passed. One might expect that in the dire circumstances of Jeremiah's day they might change, but the prophet is told that once again 'they will not listen to you'. The sincerity which comes with listening to the word of God has vanished.

> **Psalm 95 (94)** The psalm contains a similar lament 'oh that you had listened'.

THIRD WEEK IN LENT

A reading from the holy gospel according to Luke (11:14-23)

Jesus was driving out a demon and it was deaf; and it happened that when the demon had gone out the deaf man spoke, and the people were amazed. But some of them said, 'It is through Beelzebul, the prince of demons, that he drives demons out.' Others asked him, as a test, for a sign from heaven; but, knowing what they were thinking, he said to them, 'Every kingdom divided against itself is laid waste, and house collapses against house. So, too, with Satan: if he is divided against himself, how can his kingdom stand? – since you claim that it is through Beelzebul that I drive demons out. Now if it is through Beelzebul that I drive demons out, through whom do your own people drive them out? Therefore they shall be your judges. But if it is through the finger of God that I drive out demons, then the kingdom of God has caught you unawares. So long as a strong man fully armed guards his own home, his goods are undisturbed; but when someone stronger than himself attacks and defeats him, the stronger man takes away all the weapons he relied on and shares out his spoil. Anyone who is not with me is against me; and anyone who does not gather in with me throws away.'

JESUS IS ON THE way to Jerusalem, and differences with his opponents are sharpened. Some deliberately undermine the healing work of Jesus, attributing it to the work of 'Beelzebul', one of many names given to Satan. Jesus uses the analogy of a divided kingdom, and a divided household to point out the fault in their argument. The one who undermines the work of Satan cannot be said to be in league with Satan. In fact, it is by 'the finger of God' that Jesus casts out demons, and such actions are signs that the kingdom of God has drawn near. Jesus goes on to speak of himself as 'the stronger one', echoing what John the Baptist said of him (Luke 3:16). With such strength he is able to confront and vanquish Satan.

Do I ever misrepresent the works of a good person in order to undermine them?
Pray for those whose hearts are closed, and whose minds are stuck.

FRIDAY OF THE THIRD WEEK IN LENT

A reading from the prophet Hosea (14:2-10)

Israel, come back to the LORD your God!
Your guilt was the cause of your downfall.
Provide yourself with words and come back to the LORD.
Say to him, 'Take away all our guilt
and give us what is good
and we will offer the fruit of our lips.
Assyria cannot save us,
we will not ride horses any more
or say, "Our God!" to the work of our hands,
for in you orphans find compassion.'
I shall cure them of their disloyalty,
I shall love them freely,
for my anger has turned away from them.
I shall be like dew on Israel;
he will bloom like the lily
and thrust out roots like the cedar of Lebanon.
He will put out new shoots;
he will have the beauty of the olive tree
and the fragrance of Lebanon.
They will come back to live in my shade;
they will grow wheat again, they will blossom like the vine,
their wine will be as famous as the wine of Lebanon.
What has Ephraim to do with idols any more
when I hear him and watch over him?
I am like an evergreen cypress:
you owe your fruitfulness to me.
Let the wise understand these words,
let the intelligent grasp their meaning,
for the LORD's ways are straight
and the righteous will walk in them
but sinners will stumble.

THIRD WEEK IN LENT

HOSEA ADDRESSES THE NORTHERN kingdom of Israel, which split from Judah two centuries earlier. Their future is uncertain. Despite this Hosea brings the word of the Lord, who calls the people back. They have trusted for too long in alliances with pagan nations such as Assyria, and dabbled in the worship of idols. The tenderness of God of which the prophet speaks owes much to his own experience as a loyal husband who offers love and forgiveness to his unfaithful wife. God will descend like dew, describing the new condition of the people with rich natural images, such as the lily, the cedar and the olive. God in turn is like an 'evergreen cypress'. The final words of this reading, which are the last words of the book of Hosea, are an insistent invitation to the wise to heed and understand these words.

> **Psalm 81 (80)** This psalm presents words of God to the people, inviting a new start, and feeding Israel with finest wheat and wild honey.

A reading from the holy gospel according to Mark (12:28-34)

One of the scribes who had heard them debating appreciated that Jesus had given them a good answer, and put a further question to him, 'Which is the first of all the commandments?' Jesus replied, 'This is the first: Listen, Israel, the Lord our God is the one Lord, and you shall love the Lord your God with all your heart, and with all your soul, with all your mind and with all your strength. The second is this: You shall love your neighbour as yourself. There is no commandment greater than these.' The scribe said to him, 'Well spoken, teacher; what you have said is true, that he is one and there is no other. To love him with all your heart, with all your understanding and strength, and to love your neighbour as yourself, this is far more important than whole burnt offerings and sacrifices.' Jesus, seeing that he had answered wisely, said, 'You are not far from the kingdom of God.' And after that no one dared to question him any more.

THIS DIALOGUE WITH A scribe who was positively impressed by Jesus' teaching sets a more cordial tone in Jesus' discussions with religious leaders in Jerusalem. In answer to the scribe's question about 'the first of all the commandments' Jesus quotes the *shema* and its command to love God (Deuteronomy 6) to which he adds the command to love neighbour (Leviticus 19). The scribe compliments Jesus on his reply, and Jesus, 'seeing that he had answered wisely', tells him that he is 'not far from the kingdom of God'. The encounter of these two minds illustrates the profound accord of Jesus with the tradition, and not surprisingly, at least for the moment, 'no one dared to question him any more'.

Reflect on the deep bonds of Christian faith with our Jewish roots. We pray for the wisdom and courage to take up the call to repentance.

SATURDAY OF THE THIRD WEEK IN LENT

A reading from the book of the prophet Hosea (5:15-6:6)

'Come, let us return to the Lord.
He has torn us apart and he will heal us;
he has struck us and he will bind up our wounds.
After two days he will revive us,
on the third day he will raise us up
and we shall live in his presence.
Let us know, let us strive to know the Lord.
His coming is as sure as the dawn.
He will come to us like a shower,
like the rain of springtime on the earth.'
'What am I to do with you, Ephraim?
What am I to do with you, Judah?
For your love is like morning mist,
like the dew that quickly disappears.
Therefore have I hacked them to pieces
by means of the prophets,
I have killed them with words from my mouth,
my judgement will blaze forth like the light,

THIRD WEEK IN LENT

for my pleasure is in faithful love, not sacrifice,
knowledge of God, not burnt offerings.

THERE ARE TWO SPEECHES in this reading. The people begin by voicing their determination to 'return' to the Lord. The 'third day' is a metaphor for the arrival of God's salvation. The people are convinced that God will come. But is this commitment of the people genuine, or mere words? A second speech, this time of God, begins: 'What am I to do with you, Ephraim? What am I to do with you Judah?' The Lord is anxious both about the northern kingdom, Israel, also known as Ephraim, and about the southern kingdom of Judah. God's concern is that the people's love is fickle. God is frustrated by the inconstancy of the people, whose love (*hesed*) is like mist, like dew which does not last. There has been so much disappointment. Hosea draws on his own personal experience to voice the anxiety that God feels about the relationship. What God desires is faithful love (*hesed*), and knowledge of God. The offering of sacrifices is worthless without these. God is still anxiously waiting.

> **Psalm 51 (50)** The *Miserere* is used again with its penitential tones. The verses concerning true sacrifice tie up with the reading from Hosea.

A reading from the holy gospel according to Luke (18:9-14)

Jesus spoke the following parable to some people who prided themselves on being righteous, and despised everyone else, 'Two men went up to the Temple to pray, one a Pharisee, the other a tax collector. The Pharisee stood there and said this prayer to himself, "I thank you, God, that I am not grasping, unjust, adulterous like everyone else, and particularly that I am not like this tax collector here. I fast twice a week; I pay tithes on all I possess." The tax collector stood at a distance, not daring even to raise his eyes to heaven; but he beat his breast and said, "God, be merciful to me, a sinner." This man, I tell you, went home again justified; the other did not. For everyone who raises himself up will be humbled, but anyone who humbles himself will be raised up.'

READING THE BIBLE THROUGH LENT

THE ISSUE IN THE mind of Jesus is that of people who 'pride themselves' on being 'righteous'. The parable is for them. At the end of the parable we will be told who was righteous in the eyes of God. The first man, who happens to be a Pharisee, is described as 'praying to himself'. He is more concerned to denigrate 'this tax-collector here', whom he judges unrighteous, and quickly draws attention to his own virtuous deeds of fasting and tithe-paying. The second man, the tax-collector, raises his eyes to God and seeks God's mercy. All he knows of righteousness is that he stands in need of it. It is not by works that we are saved, and certainly not by pride in our works, but by humble reliance on the mercy of God. The parable should leave no doubt in the minds of the 'righteous' who 'despised everyone else'.

Do good works contribute to being righteous before God?
For those who are trapped in a judgemental mind-set, we pray.

Fourth Week in Lent

FOURTH SUNDAY OF LENT – YEAR A

A reading from the first book of Samuel (16:1, 6-7, 10-13)

The LORD said to Samuel, 'How long are you going to mourn over Saul, as I myself have rejected him as king of Israel? Fill your horn with oil and go. I am sending you to Jesse of Bethlehem, for I have found myself a king from among his sons.' When they arrived, he looked at Eliab and thought, 'Surely this is the LORD's anointed before him now,' but the LORD said to Samuel, 'Take no notice of his appearance or his height, for I have rejected him; God does not see as human beings see; they look at appearances, but the LORD looks at the heart.' So Jesse presented seven of his sons to Samuel, but Samuel said to Jesse, 'The LORD has not chosen these.' Then he asked Jesse, 'Are these all the sons you have?' Jesse replied, 'There is still one more, the youngest; he is looking after the sheep.' So Samuel said to Jesse, 'Send for him, for we shall not sit down to eat until he arrives.' Jesse had him sent for; he had ruddy cheeks, with fine eyes and an attractive appearance. The LORD said, 'Get up and anoint him: he is the one!' At this, Samuel took the horn of oil and anointed him, surrounded by his brothers; and the spirit of the LORD seized on David from that day onwards.

SAUL, THE FIRST TO be anointed king by Samuel, has proved unable to bear the burden of kingship (1 Samuel 15). The choice of David to be king, in succession to Saul, is significant not only because of the importance of David in the history of Israel. When Samuel enters the house of Jesse in Bethlehem the other sons of Jesse appeared more suitable, but God does not choose them. The story told here also teaches that God chooses not the most obvious candidate from external appearance or stature. God 'looks at the heart'. David's heart was ready to receive the spirit of the Lord. Anointing with oil is a sign of strength and consecration. David becomes an 'anointed one' (*mashiah*), like Saul before him.

> **Psalm 23 (22)** The Lord, as shepherd, provides for the needs of the people, preparing a banquet and anointing their heads with oil.

A reading from the letter of St Paul to the Ephesians (5:8-14)

Once you were darkness, but now you are light in the Lord; live as children of light, for the fruit of the light consists in complete goodness and righteousness and truth. Approve what is pleasing to the Lord. Take no part in the fruitless works of darkness but rather show them up. For what is done in secret by such people is shameful even to mention; but anything shown up by the light will be illuminated and anything illuminated is itself a light. That is why it is said:

Wake up, sleeper,
rise from the dead,
and Christ will shine on you.

THESE WORDS OF THE letter to the Ephesians on light and darkness prepare for the sign of the man born blind, receiving light from Christ. Christian baptism is also known as an enlightenment, and Christians are anointed, as David was, for a special mission. The words are directed to Christians who once lived in darkness but who through conversion and baptism have abandoned their pagan past and been joined to Christ. They are encouraged to remain faithful. We hear about the 'fruit of light': goodness, righteousness and truth, while darkness brings only 'fruitless works'. The passage ends with what is considered part of an ancient Christian hymn referring to the new life of baptism.

A reading from the holy gospel according to John (9:1-41)

As he went along, Jesus saw a man who had been blind from birth. His disciples asked him, 'Rabbi, who sinned, this man or his parents, that he was born blind?' Jesus replied, 'Neither he nor his parents sinned. He was born blind so that the works of God might be revealed in him.

'As long as day lasts
we must carry out the work of the one who sent me.
Night is coming when no one can work.

FOURTH WEEK IN LENT

As long as I am in the world
I am the light of the world.'
Having said this, he spat on the ground, made a paste with the saliva, spread it on the man's eyes, and said to him, 'Go and wash in the Pool of Siloam' (which means 'Sent'). So he went off and washed and came back able to see.

His neighbours and people who had earlier seen that he was a beggar said, 'Is not this the man who used to sit and beg?' Some said, 'It is.' Others said, 'No, but he is like the man.' The man himself said, 'Yes, I am the one.' So they said to him, 'Then how were your eyes opened?' He answered, 'The man called Jesus made a paste, spread it on my eyes and said to me, "Go off and wash at Siloam." So I went and washed and could see.' They said to him, 'Where is he?' He answered, 'I do not know.'

They brought to the Pharisees the man who had been blind. It had been a Sabbath when Jesus made the paste and opened the man's eyes, so the Pharisees asked him again how he had come to see. He said to them, 'He put a paste on my eyes, and I washed, and I can see.' Then some of the Pharisees said, 'That man is not from God: he does not keep the Sabbath.' Others said, 'How can a sinner produce such signs?' And there was division among them. So they said to the blind man again, 'What have you to say about him – as it was your eyes he opened?' The man answered, 'He is a prophet.'

However, the Jews would not believe that the man had been blind and had come to see till they had sent for the parents of the man who had come to see and asked them, 'Is this man your son whom you say was born blind? If so, how can he now see?' His parents answered, 'We know that he is our son and that he was born blind, but how he can see, we do not know, nor who opened his eyes. Ask him. He is of age: he will speak for himself.' His parents said this because they were afraid of the Jews, for the Jews had already agreed that anyone who acknowledged Jesus as the Messiah should be banned from the synagogue. This was why his parents said, 'He is of age: ask him.'

So the Jews sent a second time for the man who had been blind and said to him, 'Give glory to God! We know that this man is a sinner.' He answered, 'Whether he is a sinner I don't know; one thing I do know is that though I was blind I can now see.' They said to him, 'What did he do to you? How did he open your eyes?' He replied, 'I have told you already and you did not listen. Why do you want to hear it again? Do you want to become his disciples yourselves?' At this they hurled abuse at him, 'You are his disciple, we are disciples of Moses. We know that God has spoken to Moses, but as for this man, we do not know where he comes from.' The man replied, 'The amazing thing is this: that you do not know where he comes from and he has opened my eyes! We know that God does not listen to sinners, but God does listen to someone who reveres God and does his will. Ever since the world began it is unheard of that anyone should open the eyes of someone born blind; if this man were not from God, he would not have been able to do anything.' They answered and said to him, 'You were born wholly in sin, and are you teaching us?' And they drove him out.

Jesus heard they had driven him out, and when he had found him he said, 'Do you believe in the Son of man?' He replied, 'And who is he, sir, that I may believe in him?' Jesus said to him, 'You have seen him, and he is the one speaking to you.' He said, 'Lord, I believe,' and worshipped him.

And Jesus said:
'For judgement I came into this world,
so that those who cannot see might see,
and those who can see might become blind.'

Hearing this, some of the Pharisees who were with him said to him, 'Surely we are not blind, are we?' Jesus replied:
'If you were blind
you would not be to blame,
but since you say,
"We can see," your guilt remains.'

THIS IS THE SECOND of the three great readings from the Fourth Gospel which prepare for the reception of baptism at Easter. Last week we heard proclaimed the story of the woman at the well, and next Sunday we will hear of the raising of Lazarus. At the very beginning of this story, before he heals the man born blind, Jesus proclaims: 'As long as I am in the world I am the light of the world.' The physical healing of the man triggers a spiritual journey into light, which is in contrast to the darkness of those who cannot see the truth. This lively and honest character, who has no name, refers to Jesus as 'the man called Jesus', then 'a prophet', recognising him as 'from God' and finally worshipping him as 'Lord'.

While he is willing to receive the light, the religious authorities are not convinced, for Jesus has worked the healing on the Sabbath. They interrogate his parents to no avail. Their pestering of the man leads to his indignant question: 'Do you want to become his disciples yourselves?' Despite their abuse he is undaunted and his defence of the man 'from God' becomes more strident. They banish him from the synagogue, and remain fixed in their conviction that they themselves know all there is to know, and have seen all there is to see. The tender final encounter with Jesus leads the man to worship him with the words 'Lord, I believe.'

How effective is light as a metaphor for faith?
Pray for those who begin to sense the light in the darkness of life.

FOURTH SUNDAY OF LENT – YEAR B

A reading from the second book of Chronicles (36:14-16, 19-23)

All the leaders of Judah, the priests and the people too, added infidelity to infidelity, by all the shameful practices of the nations and by defiling the Temple of the LORD which he himself had consecrated in Jerusalem. The LORD, God of their ancestors, continually sent word to them through his messengers because he felt compassion for his people and his Dwelling, but they mocked the messengers of God, they despised his words, they laughed at his prophets, until the LORD's wrath with his people became so fierce that there was no remedy.

The king of Babylon burned down the Temple of God, demolished the walls of Jerusalem, burned all its palaces to the ground and destroyed everything of value in it. And those who had escaped the sword he deported to Babylon, where they were slaves to him and his descendants until the rise of the kingdom of Persia, to fulfil the LORD's prophecy in the mouth of Jeremiah: Until the country has paid off its Sabbaths, it will lie fallow for all the days of its desolation – to complete seventy years.

In the first year of Cyrus king of Persia – to fulfil the word of the LORD in the mouth of Jeremiah – the LORD roused the spirit of Cyrus king of Persia to send an announcement throughout his kingdom and also in writing, saying, 'Cyrus king of Persia says this, "The LORD, the

God of Heaven, has given me all the kingdoms of the earth and has appointed me to build him a Temple in Jerusalem, which is in Judah. Whoever there is among you of all his people, may the LORD his God be with him! Let him go up!"'

THIS READING, FROM THE final verses of the second book of Chronicles, looks back at the disaster of the destruction of Jerusalem by the Babylonian king Nebuchadnezzar in 587 BC, and the exile in Babylon, which ended in 538 BC. These events are attributed to the 'wrath' of God at the disobedience of Israel, though they can clearly be seen as the result of poor decisions by kings of Judah and the aggressive policies of the Babylonians. Kings and priests have disregarded the voices of the prophets. Persistent refusal of the people to heed the word of God, described by Jeremiah and Ezekiel, has led to the experience of God apparently forsaking his people. But God has new plans for new life. Through the Persian king Cyrus, a man of great vision and enlightened policies, God brings about the return to the land of Israel, and a new era in the history of Israel will begin.

> **Psalm 137 (136)** The desolation of being deported to a pagan land, of destruction of all one holds dear and precious, is vividly expressed in this psalm of longing for the return to Sion.

A reading from the letter of St Paul to the Ephesians (2:4-10)

God, being rich in mercy, through the great love with which he loved us, even when we were dead by our sins, brought us to life in Christ – it is through grace that you have been saved – and raised us up with him and seated us with him in heaven, in Christ Jesus, so that for ages to come he might show the overflowing richness of his grace in his kindness towards us in Christ Jesus. For by grace you have been saved through faith, and this is not from yourselves, but is the gift of God, not by works, so that nobody may boast. We are what he made us, created in Christ Jesus for the good works which God prepared beforehand to be our way of life.

THOUGH WE WERE DEAD through sin God has raised us to new life in Christ 'through grace'. We are promised a place 'in heaven'. This grace will overflow 'for ages to come'. The fundamental teaching of Paul, that salvation comes not from anything we might do but as a grace of God through faith, is clearly stated. Christians are thus 'created in Christ Jesus' for good works. The passage is dominated by threefold use of the word 'grace' (*charis*), the free giving of God, by which we are drawn into new life, and by the repeated use of the phrase 'in Christ Jesus'.

A reading from the holy gospel according to John (3:14-21)

Jesus said to Nicodemus:

> 'As Moses lifted up the snake in the desert,
> so must the Son of man be lifted up
> so that everyone who believes in him
> may have eternal life.
> For God loved the world so much
> that he gave his only-begotten Son,
> so that everyone who believes in him
> may not perish but may have eternal life.
> For God sent his Son into the world
> not to judge the world,
> but so that the world might be saved through him.
> One who believes in him will not be judged;
> but whoever does not believe is judged already,
> for not believing in the name of God's only-begotten Son.
> And the judgement is this:
> that the light has come into the world
> and people loved darkness rather than light
> because their deeds were evil.
> And indeed, everybody who does wrong
> hates the light and does not come to the light,
> so that such actions may not be examined.
> But whoever does the truth comes to the light,
> so that it may be clearly seen
> that this person's works have been done in God.'

THIS IMPORTANT TEXT IS part of the dialogue of Jesus with the Pharisee Nicodemus, who came to Jesus by night. Later in the gospel Nicodemus will assist with the burial of Jesus (John 19). Jesus refers to the plague of serpents suffered by Israel in the desert (Numbers 21). Like the serpent in the desert he will be 'lifted up' to give life. That 'God so loved the world that he gave his only-begotten Son', and that we are saved by faith in him, gives great consolation to Christians. It is not God who judges us, for we judge ourselves by welcoming the light and living by it. 'Doing the truth' is equivalent to walking in the light.

How do we keep the light shining in the darkness of history?
For an appreciation of the love of God, and God's light around us, we pray.

FOURTH SUNDAY OF LENT – YEAR C

A reading from the book of Joshua (5:9-12)

Then the LORD said to Joshua, 'Today I have taken the shame of Egypt away from you.' The Israelites pitched their camp at Gilgal and kept the Passover there on the fourteenth day of the month, at evening, in the plain of Jericho. On the very next day after the Passover, they ate the produce of the land: unleavened bread and roasted ears of corn. The manna stopped the day after they had eaten the produce of the land. From that year onwards the Israelites no longer had manna, but ate the produce of Canaan.'

AFTER THE FORTY YEARS of wandering in the desert the Israelites, led by Joshua, have crossed the Jordan river and entered the promised land (Joshua 3). At Gilgal Joshua circumcised those males who had not undergone this ritual during the desert years. Thus 'the shame of Egypt' is removed. Living from the produce of the land is another significant stage in the story of Israel. The time of wandering is finished, and there is no longer the need to gather manna in the desert. The Israelites are described as celebrating both Passover, the feast of a liberated people, and eating unleavened bread from the land they have entered. These two actions will become annual observances for them.

> **Psalm 34 (33)** This psalm celebrates 'tasting' and 'seeing', further metaphors for God's expected gifts.

FOURTH WEEK IN LENT

A reading from the second letter of St Paul to the Corinthians (5:17-21)

Anyone who is in Christ is a new creation. The old things have passed away; see, they have become new. Everything is from God, who reconciled us to himself through Christ, and gave us the ministry of reconciliation, because God was in Christ, reconciling the world to himself, not reckoning their sins to them, and entrusting to us the message of reconciliation. Therefore we are ambassadors for Christ, since God is appealing through us: on Christ's behalf we beg you, be reconciled to God. He who knew no sin he made sin for our sake, so that in him we might become the righteousness of God.

BEING 'IN CHRIST' BRINGS a 'new creation'. God has 'reconciled' (*katalassein*) us. 'Reconcile' or 'reconciliation' appear five times in this short passage. This reconciliation with God brings forgiveness of sin and the entrusting of a mission of reconciliation. Christians are delegated to let others know of this reconciliation, which each person embraces through faith. Christ, who knew no sin, was 'made sin' by God, lowering himself to reveal the love God has for us. We thereby become 'the righteousness of God' in him.

A reading from the holy gospel according to Luke (15:1-3, 11-32)

The tax collectors and sinners, however, were all crowding round to listen to him, and the Pharisees and scribes complained saying, 'This man welcomes sinners and eats with them.' So he told them this parable.

'There was a man who had two sons. The younger one said to his father, "Father, let me have the share of the estate that will come to me." So the father divided the property between them. A few days later, the younger son got together everything he had and left for a distant country where he squandered his money in loose living.

'When he had spent it all, that country experienced a severe famine, and now he began to be in need; so he hired himself out to one of the local inhabitants who sent him into the fields to feed the pigs. And he would willingly have filled himself with the pods which the pigs were eating, but no one would let him have them. Then he came to his senses and said, "How many of my father's hired men have all the food they want and more, and here am I dying of hunger! I will get up and go to my father and say: Father, I have sinned against heaven and against you; I no longer deserve to be called your son; treat me as one of your hired men." So he got up and went back to his father.

'While he was still a long way off, his father saw him and was moved with pity. He ran to the boy, clasped him in his arms and kissed him. Then his son said, "Father, I have sinned against heaven and against you. I no longer deserve to be called your son." But the father said to his servants, "Quick! Bring out the best robe and put it on him; put a ring on his finger and sandals on his feet. Bring the fattened calf, and kill it; we will celebrate by having a feast, because this son of mine was dead and has come back to life; he was lost and is found." And they began to celebrate.

'Now the elder son was out in the fields, and on his way back, as he drew near the house, he heard music and dancing. Calling one of the servants he asked what it was all about. The servant told him, "Your brother has come, and your father has killed the fattened calf because he has got him back safe and sound." He was angry then and refused to go in, and his father came out and began to plead with him; but he retorted to his father, "Look! All these years I have slaved for you and never disobeyed your orders, yet you never gave me so much as a young goat for me to celebrate with my friends. But, for this son of yours, when he comes back after swallowing up your property with prostitutes you kill the fattened calf." Then the father said, "My son, you are with me always and all I have is yours. But it was only right we should celebrate and rejoice, because your brother here was dead and has come to life; he was lost and is found."'

THE PARABLE OF THE 'prodigal son' illustrates what reconciliation with God means. The father offers his troublesome son a warm embrace, a new robe, and a feast. This is a drama of death and life: he was dead but is now alive. It prepares for the paschal drama. Christ enters into death so that we in him can be raised to the fullness of life. We must remain hopeful that the elder brother, and many like him, will understand the dynamic of love offered to all those who need it. They need a new heart in which forgiveness of the sinner is central. It is for those who begrudge God's mercy that the parables of Luke 15 were created.

How can we feel the merciful righteousness of God in our hearts?
Pray for those whose religious lives are blighted by rigidity and pride.

FOURTH WEEK IN LENT

MONDAY OF THE FOURTH WEEK IN LENT

A reading from the prophet Isaiah (65:17-21)
Thus says the Lord:
'Look, I am going to create new heavens and a new earth,
the past will not be remembered
and will no more come to mind.
Rather be joyful, be glad for ever at what I am creating;
for see, I am creating Jerusalem to be joy
and my people to be gladness.
I shall rejoice in Jerusalem
and take delight in my people.
The sound of weeping shall not be heard there, nor the sound of a
    shriek.
No child shall there be who lives but a few days,
nor an ancient who does not live the full span of life:
for to die at one hundred will be youthful,
the sinner's death at one hundred, a curse.
They will build houses and live in them,
plant vineyards and eat their fruit.'

THIS READING FROM THE final chapters of the book of Isaiah looks forward to 'new heavens and a new earth' with a threefold use of the word 'create' (*bara'*). These words of a post-exilic prophet anticipate a new creation, new gifts of God. They are full of joy and delight. The city of God will be rebuilt, not only the historical city, but the definitive place of God among us. Cries of pain will be no more. Children will grow to maturity. The old will expect to live beyond one hundred years. The building of houses and the growing of vines speak of the idyllic environment to come. Such is God's response to Jerusalem's cries for help.

> **Psalm 30 (29)** The psalm speaks of the same transformation from weeping to dancing. God raises up his people, both now and for ever.

READING THE BIBLE THROUGH LENT

A reading from the holy gospel according to John (4:43-54)

When the two days were over, Jesus left there for Galilee, for Jesus himself had borne witness that a prophet is not honoured in his own country. On his arrival the Galileans received him well, having seen all that he had done in Jerusalem during the festival, for they too had attended the festival.

He came again to Cana in Galilee, where he had changed the water into wine. And there was a royal official whose son was ill at Capernaum; hearing that Jesus had come from Judaea to Galilee, he went and asked him to come down and cure his son, as he was at the point of death. Jesus said to him, 'Unless you see signs and portents you will not believe!' The official said to him, 'Sir, come down before my child dies.' Jesus said to him, 'Go, your son is living.' The man believed what Jesus had said and went on his way; and while he was still on the way his slaves met him with the news that his boy was alive. He asked them when the boy had begun to recover. They replied, 'Yesterday in the early afternoon the fever left him.' The father realised that this was the time when Jesus had said, 'Your son is living'; and he and all his household believed.

This was the second sign that Jesus did, having come from Judaea to Galilee.

AFTER SPENDING TWO DAYS in a Samaritan town, Jesus travels on to Galilee and is well received. This second 'sign' of Jesus in the Fourth Gospel concerns the son of a 'royal official' with strong faith in the healing power of Jesus. Being in the royal service, presumably therefore associated with Herod Antipas, the official may be Jew or Gentile. Whatever his background he is a person who is open to faith, and is not put off by Jesus' initial rebuttal: 'Unless you see signs and portents you will not believe!' The official insists that Jesus should come to heal his son, but nevertheless believes the word of Jesus: 'your son is living.' Jesus heals even from a distance, and the official brings his whole family to faith. Their traumatic experience bound them together in hope, and now binds them in faith and love too.

Do we appreciate the faith of people of different origins and beliefs? For those desperate for the health and safety of their children, we pray.

FOURTH WEEK IN LENT

TUESDAY OF THE FOURTH WEEK IN LENT

A reading from the prophet Ezekiel (47:1-9, 12)

The man brought me back to the entrance of the Temple where a stream was flowing eastwards from under the Temple threshold, for the Temple faced east. The water was flowing from under the right side of the Temple, south of the altar. He took me out by the north gate and led me right round outside as far as the outer east gate where the water was flowing out on the right-hand side. The man went off to the east holding his measuring line and measured off four hundred metres; he then made me wade across the stream: the water reached my ankles. He measured off another four hundred metres and made me wade across the stream again: the water reached my knees. He measured off another four hundred metres and made me wade across the stream again: the water reached my waist. He measured off another four hundred metres: it was now a river which I could not cross; the stream had swollen and was now deep water, a river impossible to cross. Then he said, 'Do you see, son of man?' Then he took me and brought me back to the bank on the river. Now, when I reached it, there was an enormous number of trees on each bank of the river. He said, 'This water flows east down to the Arabah and to the sea; and flowing into the sea it makes its waters wholesome. Wherever the river flows, all living creatures teeming in it will live. Fish will be very plentiful, for wherever the water goes it brings health, and life teems wherever the river flows. Along the river, on either bank, will grow every kind of fruit tree with leaves that never wither and fruit that never fails; they will bear new fruit every month because this water comes from the sanctuary. And their fruit will be good for eating and their leaves for healing.'

A SERIES OF VISIONS, marking the return after the exile, brings the book of the prophet Ezekiel to an end. He has been given instructions about the rebuilding of the temple, and has witnessed the return of the Lord (Ezekiel 43). This further vision of the temple, rebuilt after destruction by the Babylonians, shows it to be a source of blessing and fertility, for God is there. The water gushing from the temple, in ever greater abundance, transforms the barren natural environment on the way down to the Dead Sea. Where there were only lifeless minerals new life teems. Fish are now 'very plentiful'. All along the banks there are fruit trees which 'bear new fruit every month', and have healing powers. The water from the temple speaks of God's transforming presence and prepares for Christian baptism.

> **Psalm 46 (45)** The psalm reflects the vision of Ezekiel, for the 'waters of a river' bring joy to the city of God.

A reading from the holy gospel according to John (5:1-3, 5-16)

After this there was a festival of the Jews, and Jesus went up to Jerusalem. Now in Jerusalem next to the Sheep Gate there is a pool, called Bethesda in Hebrew, which has five porticoes; and under these lay many sick people, blind, lame, paralysed. One man there had an illness which had lasted thirty-eight years, and when Jesus saw him lying there and knew he had been there for a long time, he said, 'Do you want to be well again?' The sick man replied, 'Sir, I have no one to put me into the pool when the water is disturbed; and while I am on my way, someone else gets down before me.' Jesus said, 'Get up, pick up your mat and walk around.' The man was cured at once, and picked up his mat and started to walk around.

Now that day was a Sabbath, so the Jews said to the man who had been cured, 'It is the Sabbath; you are not allowed to carry your mat.' He replied to them, 'The man who cured me said to me, "Pick up your mat and walk around."' They asked, 'Who is the man who said to you, "Pick it up and walk around"?' The man who had been healed had no idea who it was, since Jesus had disappeared, as the place was crowded. After this Jesus found him in the Temple and said, 'See, you are well again; do not sin any more, or something worse may happen to you.' The man went back and told the Jews that it was Jesus who had cured him. Therefore the Jews began to persecute Jesus because he did things like this on the Sabbath.

THIS IS ONE OF several visits of Jesus to Jerusalem in the Fourth Gospel. It seems that the pool was an ancient pagan site for healing, dedicated to the Greek god Asclepius. Jesus is present in Jerusalem for an unspecified 'festival of the Jews'. The man who has been ill for thirty-eight years is understandably despondent. There is no expression of faith or even of hope. But Jesus puts the man's well-being first, violating the Sabbath on his behalf. There is no response from the man, so that it is not surprising that Jesus chides him with 'do not sin any more, or something worse may happen to you'. This should not be understood as a threat, but perhaps simply a challenge to gratitude for his new condition. The complaint that Jesus worked the sign on the Sabbath will give rise to a lengthy exchange with certain Jews, and to the 'persecution' of Jesus.

Jesus heals this poor man despite his hopelessness.
Pray for those who feel their life is pointless.

WEDNESDAY OF THE FOURTH WEEK IN LENT

A reading from the book of the prophet Isaiah (49:8-15)

Thus says the LORD,
>'At the time of my good pleasure I answer you,
>on the day of salvation I help you.
>I have formed you and have appointed you
>as a covenant for the people,
>to restore the land, to return desolated properties,
>to say to prisoners, "Come out,"
>to those who are in darkness, "Show yourselves."
>Along the roadside they will graze
>and every bare height will be their pasture.
>They will never hunger or thirst,
>scorching wind and sun will never plague them;
>for he who pities them will lead them,
>will guide them to springs of water.
>I shall turn all my mountains into a road
>and my highways will be raised up.
>Look! Here they come from afar;
>look, these from the north and the west,

those from the land of Syene.'
Shout for joy, you heavens; rejoice, you earth!
Mountains, break into joyful cries!
For the LORD has consoled his people,
is taking pity on his afflicted ones.
Zion was saying,
'The LORD has abandoned me,
my lord has forgotten me.'
Can a woman forget the baby at her breast,
feel no love for the child of her womb?
Even if these were to forget, I shall not forget you.'

THIS PASSAGE COULD SERVE as a summary of the preaching of the Second Isaiah, great prophet of the exile, with the basic themes of restoration and liberation. God re-establishes his people, describing them as a 'covenant', for they will witness to God's 'salvation'. Freedom from captivity and from the darkness are announced. God provides pasture, and hunger and thirst are no more. God will lead them to springs of water. The landscape will be changed to allow for a smooth progress of the liberated people, joined by those 'from afar'. Heaven and earth, and even the mountains, are called upon to rejoice. The Lord 'has consoled' them, and the prophet has faithfully brought this message (Isaiah 40). The lament that 'the Lord has abandoned me, my lord has forgotten me' is countered with the image of a mother and baby. The Lord reassures the people: 'even if a mother were to forget, I shall not forget you.'

> **Psalm 145 (144)** This celebration of the qualities of tenderness of the Lord is reminiscent of the words to Moses in Exodus 34:6, for the Lord is 'slow to anger, rich in faithful love'.

A reading from the holy gospel according to John (5:17-30)

Jesus answered them, 'My Father still goes on working, and I am working, too.' Therefore the Jews kept seeking all the more to kill him, because not only was he breaking the Sabbath, but also by

FOURTH WEEK IN LENT

calling God his own Father he was making himself equal to God. To this Jesus replied and said to them:

    'Amen, Amen I say to you,
    on his own the Son can do nothing;
    he can do only what he sees the Father doing,
    and whatever the Father does the Son does likewise.
    For the Father loves the Son
    and shows him everything he himself does,
    and he will show him greater things than these,
    so that you will be astonished.
    For as the Father raises the dead and gives them life,
    so the Son also gives life to anyone he chooses.
    Nor does the Father judge anyone;
    he has given all judgement to the Son,
    so that all may honour the Son just as they honour the Father.
    Anyone who does not honour the Son
    does not honour the Father who sent him.
    Amen, Amen I say to you,
    whoever listens to my words, and believes in the one who sent me,
    has eternal life and is not brought to judgement
    but has passed over from death to life.
    Amen, Amen I say to you,
    the hour is coming and is now here
    when the dead will hear the voice of the Son of God,
    and those who hear it will live.
    For just as the Father has life in himself,
    so he has granted the Son also to have life in himself;
    and has granted him authority to give judgement
    because he is the Son of man.
    Do not be surprised at this, that the hour is coming
    when all who are in their graves will hear the sound of his voice
    and will come out, those who did good to the resurrection of life,
    and those who did evil to the resurrection of judgement.
    On my own I can do nothing.
    As I hear, so I judge, and my judgement is just,
    because I seek not my own will but the will of him who sent me.'

JESUS SPEAKS OF THE continuing 'work' of the Father, provoking further opposition: not only has he healed the paralysed man on the sabbath, but he has also called God his 'father'. Jesus explains: 'My Father goes on working, and I am working too.' Just as the Father 'raises the dead', so does the Son give life, as has been illustrated by this latest sign. There is no day of rest from good deeds, and the sign worked on the sabbath extends to a wretched paralysed man God's gift of freedom which is celebrated each week on the sabbath. Jesus goes on to speak of the judgement, which has been entrusted to the Son by the Father. Those who listen to the words of Jesus and believe in the 'one who sent' him, have eternal life and are not brought to judgement, but pass over from death to life. Jesus speaks of 'the resurrection of life' and 'the resurrection of judgement' (Daniel 12).

How can we join our good works to the work of God?
For those who work exclusively for selfish ends, we pray.

THURSDAY OF THE FOURTH WEEK IN LENT

A reading from the book of Exodus (32:7-14)

The LORD then said to Moses, 'Go down at once, for your people whom you brought up from the land of Egypt have gone wrong. They have been quick to leave the way that I ordered them to follow. They have cast themselves an image of a calf, worshipped it and offered sacrifice to it, shouting, "These are your gods, Israel, who brought you up from the land of Egypt!"'

The LORD said to Moses, 'I have seen this people. Look how obstinate they are! So leave me now, so that my anger can blaze at them and I make an end of them! I shall make you into a great nation instead.'

Moses tried to pacify the LORD his God and said, 'Why, LORD, does your anger blaze at your people, whom you have brought out of the land of Egypt by your great power and mighty hand? Why should the Egyptians say, "He brought them out with evil intention, to slaughter them in the mountains and wipe them off the face of the earth?" Give up your burning wrath; relent over this disaster for your people. Remember your servants Abraham, Isaac and Jacob, to whom you swore by yourself and made this promise, "I shall make your descendants as numerous as the stars of heaven, and this whole country of which I have spoken, I shall give to your descendants, and it will be their heritage for ever."' The LORD then relented over the disaster which he had intended for his people.

AFTER FORTY DAYS MOSES comes down Mount Sinai to be greeted by apostasy among the people. In the absence of Moses they have prevailed upon Aaron to cast an idol of a golden calf, which they have worshipped. Salvation has been attributed to idols, to 'a bull which eats grass'. God threatens to unleash his 'anger', and offers a covenant to Moses instead. Moses, like Abraham before him, pleads for the people. What will the Egyptians say if God, the saviour of Israel, goes on to 'slaughter them in the mountains and wipe them off the face of the earth'? Moses recalls the promise God made with Abraham, Isaac and Jacob, of a land and innumerable offspring. And God relents.

> **Psalm 106 (105)** The psalm recounts these events in the wilderness. How could they exchange the 'bull which eats grass' for God? And yet false gods are always in fashion.

A reading from the holy gospel according to John (5:31-47)

Jesus said:
>'If I bear witness about myself, my testimony is not true;
>but there is another who witnesses about me,
>and I know that his witness about me is true.
>You sent messengers to John, and he bore witness to the truth.
>I do not accept human witness;
>it is for your salvation that I say this.
>He was the lamp burning and shining
>and for a time you were glad to rejoice in his light.
>But I have a greater witness than John's:
>the deeds my Father has given me to complete,
>these same deeds that I do witness that the Father has sent me.
>Besides, the Father who sent me himself witnesses on my behalf.
>You have never heard his voice, you have never seen his form,

and you do not have his word dwelling in you
because you do not believe in the one whom he sent.
You search the scriptures,
believing that in them you have eternal life;
it is these that bear witness about me,
and yet you are not willing to come to me to have life!
I do not accept glory from any human being,
but I know that you do not have the love of God in you.
I have come in the name of my Father and you do not accept me;
if someone else comes in his own name you will accept such a one.
How can you believe, if you accept glory from one another
but do not seek glory from God?
Do not think that I will be your accuser before the Father;
your accuser will be Moses, in whom you have put your hope.
If you believed Moses you would believe me,
for it was about me that he wrote.
If you do not believe his writings, how will you believe my words?'

THE WORDS OF JESUS after the healing of the man at the pool of Bethesda in John chapter 5 continue and conclude in this reading. He has been speaking about the work he and the Father do. Now the question is about witnesses to support his case and Jesus refers to three. The witness given by John the Baptist, a 'lamp shining for a time', was nevertheless only a 'human witness'. The 'greater' witness is 'the deeds my Father has given me to complete'. And yet deeds such as the healing of the paralysed man are rejected, because they refuse to believe 'in the one whom God sent'. They also reject the Scriptures, which 'bear witness' to Jesus. They are not willing to receive life from Jesus. They trust in Moses but Moses will become their accuser because what Moses wrote testifies to Jesus.

Are there any other witnesses to Jesus?
Pray for those whose religion does not allow them to learn new things.

FRIDAY OF THE FOURTH WEEK IN LENT

A reading from the book of Wisdom (2:12-22)

The godless say:
>'Let us lay traps for the righteous
>who annoys us and opposes our way of life,
>reproaches us for our sins against the Law
>and broadcasts our sins against our upbringing.
>Such a person claims to have knowledge of God,
>claims to be a child of the Lord,
>a reproof to our way of thinking –
>the very sight weighs us down!
>Such a life is abnormal!
>Such ways are exclusive!
>He thinks we are damaged goods
>and avoids us like filth.
>Blessing he finds in the death of the righteous
>and he boasts that God is his father.
>Let us see if what he says is true
>and test him to see what end he will have.
>For if the righteous is the son of God,
>God will hold him fast and rescue him from the grasp of his
>   enemies.
>We'll test him with insult and torture,
>find out just how gentle he is and test out that patience of his.
>We'll condemn him to a shameful death;
>he'll be looked after – he thinks!'
>This is how they reasoned but they were misled,
>for their wickedness made them blind.
>They knew not the secrets of God,
>had no hope of the reward of holiness,
>nor belief in the prize for innocence.

THIS POEM FROM THE book of Wisdom, a book which wonderfully blends Jewish thinking and Greek culture, contrasts the righteous with the godless. These latter plan to put the righteous one to the test (*peirasmos*). They are well aware what he thinks of them, and they know he is right. They resent his goodness and plan to insult and torture him. These words originate in a pagan environment, in which fidelity to the ancient faith and its values are a source of irritation. Once the speech of the godless ends the writer affirms that 'their wickedness has made them blind'. Attacks on the innocent and the just punctuate the Scriptures, and include the Just One himself and his followers in the New Testament.

> **Psalm 34 (33)** The just one trusts in God's protection.

A reading from the holy gospel according to John (7:1-2, 10, 25-30)

After this Jesus went around in Galilee, for he did not wish to go around in Judaea, because the Jews were seeking to kill him. The Jewish festival of Tabernacles was near. After his brothers had left for the festival, then he went up as well, not openly but in secret.

Meanwhile some of the people of Jerusalem were saying, 'Is not this the man they are seeking to kill? And here he is, speaking openly, and they say nothing to him! Can it be that the authorities have recognised that he is the Messiah? Yet we know where this man is from, but when the Messiah comes no one will know where he is from.'

Then, as Jesus was teaching in the Temple, he cried out:
'You know me and you know where I am from.
Yet I have not come of my own accord:
but he who sent me is true,
whom you do not know.
I know him because I am from him
and he sent me.'

So they sought to arrest him, but no one laid a hand on him because his hour had not yet come.

DURING THIS VISIT OF Jesus to Jerusalem for the feast of Tabernacles we hear more explicitly about the plots to kill him and the disputes among the people about him. The discussion focuses on his place of origin. They know he is from Galilee, but the Messiah is not supposed to be from there, and his origins might be unknown. This leads in to a solemn speech of Jesus about his real origin from the Father, and his being 'sent' by the Father. The one who sends him is 'true'. Though there is strong desire to arrest Jesus, his hour has not yet come. But it is approaching and the atmosphere becomes more and more menacing.

Note how effectively this evangelist evokes the looming danger for Jesus. Pray for all those who live under threat and in danger of violence.

SATURDAY OF THE FOURTH WEEK IN LENT

A reading from the prophet Jeremiah (11:18-20)

The LORD informed me and so I knew it; you then revealed their scheming to me. I for my part was like a trustful lamb being led to the slaughterhouse, not knowing the schemes they were plotting against me, 'Let us destroy the tree with its fruit, let us cut him off from the land of the living, so that his name is remembered no more!'

    O LORD Sabaoth whose judgement is righteous,
    you test the mind and the heart:
    let me see your vengeance upon them,
    for I have revealed my cause to you.

JEREMIAH HAS BEEN CALLED to bring an unwelcome message to his contemporaries, the urgent call to surrender to the power of Babylon. In one of his 'confessions', his outpourings in the face of the enemies who surround him, he resembles Jesus in those final days. It is the Lord who has made him aware of the danger: 'you revealed their scheming to me'. He compares himself to a lamb led unwittingly to the slaughter. They are determined to cut down this tree and to destroy its fruit. Jeremiah's prayer for God's vengeance may surprise us, and yet, he actually entrusts his 'cause' (*rib*) to God.

> **Psalm 7** The plight of the just man faced with violence, and his trust in God's protection, are the theme of this psalm.

READING THE BIBLE THROUGH LENT

A reading from the holy gospel according to John (7:40-52)

Members of the crowd who had heard these words said, 'He is truly the prophet,' others said, 'He is the Messiah,' but others said, 'Is the Messiah to come from Galilee? Does not scripture say that the Messiah is to be from the seed of David and to come from Bethlehem, the village where David was?' So there was a division in the crowd about him. Some of them wanted to arrest him, but no one laid hands on him.

The officers went back to the chief priests and Pharisees who said to them, 'Why did you not bring him?' The officers replied, 'No one has ever spoken like this man.' So the Pharisees answered them, 'Have you, too, been led astray? Have any of the authorities of the Pharisees believed in him? This crowd, which knows nothing about the Law – they are accursed.' One of them, Nicodemus – who had come to Jesus earlier – said to them, 'Surely our Law does not judge anyone without first giving that person a hearing and discovering what he is doing?' They answered and said, 'Are you a Galilean too? Search and you will see: a prophet does not arise in Galilee.'

THE PRESENCE OF JESUS in Jerusalem for the feast of Tabernacles provokes further discussion about his origins. This text shows the division among the people, some of whom declare Jesus to be the expected 'prophet', even the 'Messiah', while others oppose him. The chief priests and Pharisees are annoyed when the officers sent earlier to apprehend Jesus do not arrest him. They defend themselves: 'No one has ever spoken like this man.' The Pharisees believe they are the only ones not deceived by Jesus, but Nicodemus speaks up for a proper hearing of Jesus' case. The one who had earlier come to Jesus by night (John 3) defends him now, and will assist Joseph of Arimathaea in honouring the body of Jesus as the gospel draws towards its end (John 19).

How easy it is to dismiss those who 'know nothing', without hearing their truth!
We thank God for those who have the courage to speak the truth at considerable risk to themselves.

Fifth Week
in Lent

FIFTH SUNDAY OF LENT – YEAR A

A reading from the prophet Ezekiel (37:12-14)
Thus says the Lord God: I am now going to open your graves; I shall raise you from your graves, my people, and lead you back to the soil of Israel. And you will know that I am the Lord when I open your graves and raise you from your graves, my people, and put my spirit in you, and you shall live and I will resettle you on your own soil. Then you will know that I, the Lord, have spoken and done this – declares the Lord God.

EZEKIEL'S FAMOUS VISION OF dry bones in a valley brought back to life (37:1-11) symbolised the resurgence of the nation after the long years of the Babylonian exile. The prophet, who is preaching in Babylon, now gives further encouraging words of the Lord. He uses a similar image, that of raising bodies from the grave. The whole people will receive the spirit which will renew God's life within them. And they will return to the land of Israel. The prophet stresses that Israel will 'know' that it is the Lord who brings about this life-giving intervention.

> **Psalm 130 (129)** The psalm speaks of deliverance from the 'depths', here suggesting the loss and despair which the exiled people knew in Babylon.

A reading from the letter of St Paul to the Romans (8:8-11)
Those who live by the flesh cannot be pleasing to God. You, however, are not in the flesh but in the Spirit, since the Spirit of God dwells in you. Anyone who does not have the Spirit of Christ does not belong to him. But if Christ is in you, the body is dead because of sin but the Spirit is alive because of righteousness. And if the Spirit of him who

raised Jesus from the dead dwells in you, then he who raised Christ Jesus from the dead will give life to your mortal bodies too through his Spirit dwelling in you.

THE CHRIST WHO HAS given his life for the salvation of all offers new life through baptism. The life-giving Spirit is available to the followers of Christ, who choose to live not 'in the flesh' but 'in the Spirit'. As suggested in the prophecy of Ezekiel, the Spirit is life-giving. The Spirit who raised Jesus up from death will give life to those who are baptised into Christ, even giving new life to our mortal bodies. The mystery of death and resurrection is lived out day by day.

A reading from the holy gospel according to John (11:1-45)

There was a sick man named Lazarus of Bethany, the village of Mary and her sister, Martha. It was Mary, the sister of the sick man Lazarus, who anointed the Lord with ointment and wiped his feet with her hair. The sisters sent this message to Jesus, 'Lord, the one you love is sick.' On hearing this, Jesus said, 'This sickness will not lead to death, but is for God's glory so that through it the Son of God may be glorified.'

Jesus loved Martha and her sister and Lazarus, yet when he heard that he was sick he stayed where he was for two more days. Then after this he said to the disciples, 'Let us go back to Judaea.' The disciples said, 'Rabbi, just now the Jews were trying to stone you; are you going back there again?' Jesus replied:

'Are there not twelve hours in the day?
No one who walks in the daytime stumbles,
having the light of this world to see by;
anyone who walks around at night stumbles,
having no light as a guide.'

He said that and then added, 'Our friend Lazarus is at rest; I am going to wake him up.' The disciples said to him, 'Lord, if he is at rest he will be saved.' Jesus had been speaking of the death of Lazarus, but they thought that by 'rest' he meant sleep. So Jesus put it plainly, 'Lazarus has died; and for your sake I am glad I was not there, so that you may believe. But let us go to him.' Then Thomas – known as the Twin – said to the other disciples, 'Let us also go to die with him.'

FIFTH WEEK IN LENT

On arriving, Jesus found that Lazarus had been in the tomb for four days already. Bethany is only about three kilometres from Jerusalem, and many Jews had come to Martha and Mary to comfort them about their brother. When Martha heard that Jesus was coming she went to meet him. Mary remained sitting in the house. Martha said to Jesus, 'Lord, if you had been here, my brother would not have died, but even now I know that God will grant whatever you ask of him.' Jesus said to her, 'Your brother will rise again.' Martha said to him, 'I know he will rise again at the resurrection on the last day.' Jesus said to her:

'I am the resurrection and life.
Anyone who believes in me,
even though that person dies, will live,
and no one who lives and believes in me will ever die.
Do you believe this?'

She said, 'Yes, Lord. I believe that you are the Messiah, the Son of God, the one coming into this world.'

When she had said this, she went and called her sister Mary, saying quietly, 'The Master is here and is calling you.' Hearing this, Mary got up quickly and went to him. Jesus had not yet come into the village; he was still at the place where Martha had met him. The Jews who were in the house comforting Mary, seeing her get up quickly and go out, followed her, thinking that she was going to the tomb to weep there. When Mary came to where Jesus was, seeing him she fell at his feet, saying, 'Lord, if you had been here, my brother would not have died.' When Jesus saw her weeping, and the Jews who had come with her also, he was distressed in spirit, and profoundly moved. He said, 'Where have you laid him?' They said, 'Lord, come and see.' Jesus wept; and the Jews said, 'See how he loved him!' Some of them said, 'Could not he who opened the eyes of the blind man have prevented this man from dying?' Again inwardly distressed, Jesus reached the tomb: it was a cave, closed by a stone. Jesus said, 'Take the stone away.' Martha, the dead man's sister, said to him, 'Lord, there is already a stench; he has been dead for four days.' Jesus replied, 'Have I not told you that if you believe you will see the glory of God?' So they took the stone away. Then Jesus lifted up his eyes and said:

'Father, I thank you for hearing my prayer.
I myself knew that you hear me always,

but I speak
for the sake of all the crowd standing around me,
so that they may believe that you sent me.'

When he had said this, he cried in a loud voice, 'Lazarus, come out!' The dead man came out, his feet and hands bound with strips of material, and his face wrapped in a cloth. Jesus said to them, 'Unbind him, and let him go.'

Many of the Jews who had come to visit Mary, and had seen what he did, believed in him.

THE SEVENTH AND FINAL 'sign' in the Gospel of John is read as Easter approaches. It is the most obvious sign that Jesus is Lord of life. Jesus delays visiting his sick friend. His sickness, he tells the disciples, will be 'for God's glory'. When Jesus arrives in Bethany Lazarus has been in the tomb for four days. The sisters of Lazarus, Martha and Mary, express faith in different ways. Martha explicitly professes her belief in the resurrection 'on the last day', to which Jesus replies that he is 'the resurrection and life'. Martha's response is to affirm that Jesus is 'the Messiah, the Son of God, the one coming into this world'. Mary has fewer words, and her tears show her love both for her brother and for Jesus. As he approaches the tomb Jesus too weeps. His prayer to the Father is for those around him to hear, to challenge their faith. The narrative in fact concludes with the statement that after this final sign 'many' came to believe in him. Plots are then made to kill not only Jesus, but Lazarus too (12:10-11).

How is it that this sign provokes plots against Lazarus and against Jesus?
Pray for those who cannot weep.

FIFTH SUNDAY OF LENT – YEAR B

A reading from the prophet Jeremiah (31:31-34)

'Look, the days are coming – declares the LORD – when I shall make a new covenant with the House of Israel and the House of Judah, but not like the covenant I made with their ancestors the day I took them by the hand to bring them out of the land of Egypt, a covenant which they broke, even though I was their Master – declares the LORD. For this is the covenant I shall make with the House of Israel when those days have come – declares the LORD. Within them I shall plant my Law, writing it on their hearts. Then I shall be their God and they will be my people. They will no longer teach one another, saying, "Learn to know the LORD!" for they will all know me, from the least to the greatest – declares the LORD – since I shall forgive their guilt and never more call their sin to mind.'

IN THE 'BOOK OF consolation' of the prophet Jeremiah (chapters 30-33), after the disaster of the destruction of Jerusalem and of the exile, the prophet looks to the future with hope. For the first time in Scripture we hear the expression 'new covenant'. It will be made with the whole people of God, even though they broke the covenant made 'with their Master' when they left Egypt. Things will change, for this covenant, unlike the former one, will involve the Law being written on the hearts of the people. It will involve truly 'knowing' the Lord, showing justice to the poor and the needy as king Josiah did, and avoiding violence and oppression (Jeremiah 22:16-17). In the new covenant all people young and old will experience God's forgiveness.

> **Psalm 51 (50)** This penitential psalm, used so frequently throughout Lent, anticipates the washing away of guilt and the gift of a new heart and a new spirit.

A reading from the letter to the Hebrews (5:7-9)

During the days of his flesh, he offered up prayer and entreaty, with loud cries and with tears, to the one who had the power to save him from death, and, winning a hearing by his reverence, he learnt obedience, Son though he was, through his sufferings; when he had been perfected, he became for all who obey him the source of eternal salvation.

THIS READING WILL BE heard again on Good Friday. Jesus, the Son of God, the trustworthy and merciful high priest of the new covenant, by obedience gives his life to bring the human race salvation. Jesus is described, as in Gethsemane, as offering 'prayer and entreaty', remaining in contact with his God despite his dread of what lies ahead. He is the new priest of the 'order of Melchizedek', who offers his life 'once and for all' for all people. His perfect sacrifice is never to be repeated and valid for all times.

A reading from the holy gospel according to John (12:20-33)

Among those who went up to worship at the festival were some Greeks. These approached Philip, who was from Bethsaida in Galilee, and put this request to him, 'Sir, we would like to see Jesus.' Philip went to tell Andrew, and Andrew and Philip together went to tell Jesus.

Jesus replied to them:
'Now the hour has come
for the Son of man to be glorified.
Amen, Amen I say to you,
unless a wheat grain falls into the earth and dies,
it remains only a single grain;
but if it dies it bears much fruit.
Anyone who loves life loses it;
anyone who hates life in this world
will keep it for eternal life.
Whoever serves me, must follow me,
and my servant will be with me wherever I am.
Whoever serves me, my Father will honour.
Now my soul is troubled.
What shall I say:
Father, save me from this hour?
But it is for this very reason
that I have come to this hour.
Father, glorify your name!'

A voice came from heaven, 'I have glorified it, and I will again glorify it.'

The crowd standing by, who heard this, said it was thunder; others said, 'An angel has spoken to him.' Jesus answered, 'This voice came not for my sake, but for yours.

'Now is the judgement of this world,

now the ruler of this world will be driven out.
And when I am lifted up from the earth,
I shall draw all people to myself.'
Saying this he indicated the kind of death he would die.

SOME GREEKS, NON-JEWISH pagans, wish to 'see' Jesus. The disciples facilitate their meeting and Jesus, as happens so often in this gospel, gives a reply which goes well beyond their request. At Cana he had declined to anticipate the 'hour' (John 2). Now he declares that his 'hour' has indeed come, the time for him to be 'glorified'. The glory is the demonstration that the Father is with him. He speaks of the seed that must die to produce fruit, a way marked out for him and for his 'servants'. His anxiety whether he should ask to be delivered from this 'hour' recalls the anguish of the garden of Gethsemane in the other gospels. The hesitation is quickly transcended with the statement that he is ready for the 'hour'. The mysterious 'voice' from heaven may be compared to the voice heard at the Transfiguration, which commends his commitment to the cross. It is by the cross that Jesus will 'draw all people to himself'.

Do I really want to see Jesus?
Pray for those who are searching for the truth.

FIFTH SUNDAY OF LENT – YEAR C

A reading from the prophet Isaiah (43:16-21)
Thus says the Lord,
who made a way through the sea,
a path in the mighty waters,
who led out chariot and horse,
a mighty army together.
'They lay down no more to rise,
they were snuffed out, put out like a wick.
No need to remember past events,
to harp on what was done before.
Look, I am about to do something new,
now it is springing up; can you not see it?

I am making a road in the desert and rivers in wastelands.
The wild animals will honour me,
the jackals and the ostriches,
for I am giving water in the desert
and rivers through the wastelands
for my people, my chosen ones, to drink.
The people I have formed for myself will declare my praise.'

IN RESPONSE TO THE laments of the people the prophets of the exile announce that God is going to do a 'new deed'. For the Second Isaiah there is no need to recall the exodus from Egypt, when God 'made a way through the sea' and demonstrated faithful love towards the people. Now, in the depths of exile in Babylon, the Lord says 'something new' is about to be seen. Even the natural world will be changed, for God is 'making a road in the desert and rivers in wastelands' to enable the people to return home. The most unlikely creatures, jackals and ostriches, will give glory to God, for God provides water for animals and human beings, a sign of enduring care for the whole creation. If the past deeds of God were glorious, how much more glorious will be God's new deeds. Praise of God is the logical outcome, as the works of God are told to future generations.

> **Psalm 126 (125)** Liberation from slavery with joyful singing, which had been impossible during the exile (Ps 137:4), is celebrated here. Jubilation will replace tears.

A reading from the letter of St Paul to the Philippians (3:8-14)

Yes, I will go further: because of the supreme advantage of knowing Christ Jesus my Lord, I count everything else as loss. For him I have accepted the loss of all other things, and look on them all as filth if only I can gain Christ and be found in him, having not my own righteousness from the Law, but righteousness from God through faith in Christ, based on faith, that I may come to know him and the power of his resurrection, and partake of his sufferings by being moulded to the pattern of his death, if somehow I may reach the goal of resurrection from the dead.

Not that I have secured it already, nor yet reached my goal; but I am still pursuing it, in the attempt to take hold of the prize for which Christ Jesus took hold of me. Brothers and sisters, I do not reckon myself as having taken hold of it; but one thing is that forgetting all that lies behind me, and straining forward to what lies ahead, I am racing towards the finishing-point to win the prize of God's heavenly call in Christ Jesus.

PAUL WRITES TO HIS dear Philippian Christians from prison, sharing the depth of his faith and love for Christ Jesus, crucified and risen. This passage might be regarded as Paul's 'confession of faith'. His knowing Jesus is a 'supreme advantage' which makes everything else insignificant. His 'righteousness' comes not from the Law, as he once thought, but from faith in Christ, which rules out the need to justify oneself by works. Paul is clear that this journey is not over for him and lasts throughout life. Sharing in the suffering and death of Christ he longs for the resurrection. He yearns for the 'prize' of the heavenly call of God in Christ Jesus. He 'races' like an athlete towards the 'finishing-point'.

A reading from the holy gospel according to John (8:1-11)

Jesus went to the Mount of Olives.

At daybreak he appeared in the Temple again; and the whole people came to him, and he sat down and began to teach them. The scribes and Pharisees brought a woman who had been caught in adultery; and making her stand there in the middle they said to Jesus, 'Teacher, this woman has been caught in the very act of committing adultery. In the Law Moses ordered us to stone women of this kind. What do you say?' This they said testing him, so that they might have an accusation to bring against him. But Jesus bent down and started writing on the ground with his finger. When they kept on questioning him, he straightened up and said, 'Let the one among you who is without sin be the first to throw a stone at her.' Then bending down again he continued writing on the ground. When they heard this they went away one by one, beginning with the eldest, until the last one had gone and Jesus was left alone with the woman, standing in the middle. Then Jesus straightened up and said to her, 'Woman, where are they? Has no one condemned you?' She replied, 'No one, sir.' Then Jesus said, 'Neither do I condemn you. Go! And from now on do not sin again.'

THE WOMAN IN THIS gospel passage is a victim, twice over. She is a victim of whoever committed adultery with her, who has disappeared from the scene. She is then the victim of the group of religious leaders who bring her before Jesus as if for a trial. Jesus too is under threat: is he to abide by the strict letter of the Law and condemn her? Is this question, like that about taxes to Caesar, designed as a trap? The silence of Jesus is eloquent, and forces a pause. His twice 'writing on the ground' allows for hesitation, both for those driving the 'trial', and for today's reader. No one condemns the woman, and Jesus himself says: 'Neither do I condemn you.' Jesus effectively opens new life for the woman, and perhaps even for her accusers too.

What does the silence of Jesus say?
For all women who suffer, we pray.

MONDAY OF THE FIFTH WEEK IN LENT

A reading from the prophet Daniel (13:1-9, 15-17, 19-30, 33-62)

In Babylon there lived a man named Joakim. He married a woman called Susanna, daughter of Hilkiah, a woman of great beauty and one who revered God. Her parents were righteous and had instructed their daughter in the Law of Moses. Joakim was a very rich man and had a garden adjoining his house; a considerable number of the Jews used to visit him, since he was held in greater respect than anyone else.

Two elders had been elected from the people that year to act as judges. About them the Lord had said, 'Wickedness came out from Babylon from elders who were judges, who were supposed to govern the people.' These men were often at Joakim's house and all who had a case to be judged used to come to them. At midday, when the people had gone away, Susanna would take a walk in her husband's garden. The two elders used to watch her every day as she went in to take her walk and began to lust after her. They threw reason aside, making no effort to turn their eyes to heaven and forgetting the demands of virtue. So it happened that they were waiting for a favourable moment;

and one day Susanna came as usual, accompanied only by two young maidservants. The day was hot and she wanted to bathe in the garden. There was no one about except the two elders, spying on her from their hiding place. She said to the servants, 'Bring me some oil and balsam and shut the garden door while I bathe.'

Hardly were the maids gone when the two elders sprang up and rushed on her, saying, 'Look, the garden doors are shut, no one can see us. We want to have you, so agree and lie with us! Otherwise we will give evidence against you that a young man was with you and that was why you sent your maids away.' Susanna groaned and said, 'I am trapped. If I agree, it means death for me; if I refuse, I cannot escape your hands. I would rather refuse and fall into your hands than sin in the eyes of the Lord.' Then she cried out at the top of her voice. The two elders began shouting too, against her. One of them ran to open the garden doors. When the people in the house heard the shouting in the garden, they rushed out by the side entrance to see what had happened to her. Once the elders had told their story, the servants were thoroughly ashamed, because nothing of this sort had ever been said of Susanna.

Next day, as the people gathered at the house of her husband Joakim, the two elders arrived, full of their wicked plan against Susanna, to have her put to death. Before all the people they said, 'Send for Susanna daughter of Hilkiah and wife of Joakim.' She was sent for and came accompanied by her parents, her children and all her relations.

Her own people were weeping and so were all the others who saw her. The two elders stood up with all the people round them, and laid their hands on her head. Tearfully she turned her eyes to heaven, her heart confident in God. Then the elders spoke, 'While we were walking by ourselves in the garden, this woman arrived with two young maidservants. She shut the garden door and then dismissed the servants. A young man who had been hiding went over to her and lay down with her. From the corner of the garden where we were, we saw this wickedness taking place and ran towards them. Though we saw them embracing, we could not overpower the man, as he was too strong for us; he opened the door and got away. We did, however, get hold of this woman and ask her who the young man was. She refused to tell us. That is our evidence.'

Since they were elders of the people and judges, the assembly accepted their word: Susanna was condemned to death. She cried out at the top of her voice, 'Eternal God, you know all secrets and everything before it happens; you know that these men have given false evidence against me. And now I am to die, innocent as I am of everything their malice has invented against me!' The Lord heard her cry and, as she was being led away to die, he roused the holy spirit residing in a young boy called Daniel who shouted at the top of his voice, 'I am innocent of this woman's blood!' All the people turned to him and asked, 'What do you mean by that?' Standing in the middle of the crowd, he replied, 'Are you such fools, children of Israel, as to condemn a daughter of Israel without examination and without clear evidence? Go back to the scene of the trial: the evidence these men have given against her is false.'

The whole people hurried back, and the elders said to Daniel, 'Come and sit with us and explain to us, since God has given you the standing of an elder.' Daniel said, 'Keep the men well apart from each other, and I will examine them.'

When the men had been separated from each other, Daniel summoned one of them and said, 'You have grown old in wickedness and now the sins of your earlier days have caught up with you, your unjust judgements, your condemnation of the innocent, your acquittal of the guilty, although the Lord has said, "You shall not put to death the innocent and righteous." Now then, since you saw her so clearly, tell me under what sort of tree you saw them lying.' He replied, 'Under a gum tree.' Daniel said, 'Your lie deservedly recoils on your own head: the angel of God has already received your sentence from him and will cut you in half.' Putting the man to one side, he ordered the other to be brought and said to him, 'Son of Canaan, not of Judah, beauty has seduced you, lust has led your heart astray! This is how you have been behaving with the daughters of Israel and they have been so frightened that they went along with you. But now a daughter of Judah would not tolerate your wickedness! Now then, tell me under what sort of tree you caught them.' He replied, 'Under an evergreen oak tree.' Daniel said, 'Your lie deservedly recoils on your own head too: the angel of God is waiting with a sword to cut you in half and destroy the pair of you.'

FIFTH WEEK IN LENT

Then the whole assembly raised a great shout, blessing God, the Saviour of those who trust in him. And they turned on the two elders whom Daniel had convicted of false evidence out of their own mouths. As the Law of Moses prescribes, they were given the same punishment as they had schemed to inflict on their neighbour. They were put to death. And thus, that day, innocent blood was saved.

THIS STORY IS ONE OF the later additions in the Greek language to the Book of Daniel. While Daniel in the traditions of the Hebrew Bible is a visionary and interpreter of dreams, in this extra chapter of the book he is a figure of wisdom. Despite his youth he can see more clearly than others. Susanna, daughter of a righteous and God-fearing Jewish family living in Babylon, is nevertheless accused by the elders, who abuse their position of prestige in the community to satisfy their own worst desires. But wisdom triumphs through the simple ploy of the young Daniel, whose name means 'judgement of God'.

> **Psalm 23 (22)** Even though she walked in the 'valley of death' Susanna's trust in the Lord is rewarded.

In Years A and B the gospel is that for the Fifth Sunday of Lent Year C (given above).
In Year C the following gospel is read.

A reading from the holy gospel according to John (8:12-20)

Again Jesus spoke to them, saying:
>'I am the light of the world;
>anyone who follows me
>will not be walking in the dark,
>but will have the light of life.'

So the Pharisees said to him, 'You are witnessing on your own behalf; your witness is not true.' Jesus replied:
>'Even though I witness on my own behalf,
>my witness is true, because I know
>where I have come from and where I am going;

but you do not know where I come from or where I am going.
You judge by human standards; I judge no one,
but if I judge, my judgement is true,
because I am not alone, but I and the Father who sent me.
In your Law it is written
that the witness of two people is true.
I witness on my own behalf,
but the Father who sent me witnesses on my behalf, too.'
They asked him, 'Where is your Father?'
Jesus answered:
'You do not know me, nor do you know my Father;
if you did know me, you would know my Father as well.'
He spoke these words in the Treasury, while teaching in the Temple. No one arrested him, because his hour had not yet come.

JESUS IS IN JERUSALEM for the Feast of Tabernacles, which involves the lighting of candles. Jesus declares that he is 'the light of the world'. He is the light which 'darkness cannot overpower' (John 1:5). As long as he is in the world he is 'the light of the world' (John 9:5). Once again the opponents of Jesus complain that he witnesses on his own behalf. As he did after the healing of the paralysed man (John 5:31), Jesus declares that the witness on whom he relies is the Father. But the Father is not known by those to whom he is talking here: 'You do not know me, nor do you know my Father.'

We can only come to know the Father through Jesus.
Pray for those who dismiss the wisdom which comes from God through Jesus.

TUESDAY OF THE FIFTH WEEK IN LENT

A reading from the book of Numbers (21:4-9)

They left Mount Hor by the road to the Sea of Suph, to skirt round Edom. On the way the people lost patience. They spoke against God and against Moses, 'Why did you bring us up out of Egypt to die in the desert? For there is neither food nor water here; we are sick of this wretched food.' At this, God sent fiery serpents among the people; their bite brought death to many in Israel. The people came and said to Moses, 'We have sinned by speaking against the LORD and against you. Intercede for us with the LORD to save us from these serpents.' So Moses interceded for the people, and the LORD replied, 'Make a fiery serpent and raise it as a standard. Anyone who is bitten and looks at it will survive.' So Moses made a serpent out of bronze and raised it as a standard, and anyone who was bitten by a serpent and looked at the bronze serpent survived.

THE ISRAELITES CONTINUE THEIR journey through the desert led by Moses. The preservation in Scripture of the curious tale of the bronze serpent might surprise us. King Hezekiah abolished such totems and had them destroyed, including the bronze serpent mentioned explicitly in the second book of Kings (2 Kings 18). The persistence of the tradition and its preservation in the book of Numbers perhaps show moderation in understanding the manifold ways in which people can reach out for God's help, and express faith in something greater than themselves. The people acknowledge their guilt and ask Moses to intercede for them with God. It is God who tells them to 'look at the serpent', and it is God who heals.

> **Psalm 102 (101)** The psalm speaks of those condemned to die being freed.

A reading from the holy gospel according to John (8:21-30)

Again Jesus said to them:
> 'I am going away; you will look for me
> but you will die in your sin.
> Where I am going, you cannot come.'

So the Jews said to one another, 'Is he going to kill himself, that he says, "Where I am going, you cannot come?"' And he said to them:
> 'You are from below;
> I am from above.

You are of this world;
I am not of this world.
I have told you already:
you will die in your sins.
For if you do not believe that I am He,
you will die in your sins.
So they said to him, 'Who are you?' Jesus answered:
'What I have told you from the outset.
About you I have much to say
and to judge;
but the one who sent me is true,
and what I have learnt from him
I declare to the world.'
They did not recognise that he was talking to them about the Father. So Jesus said:
'When you have lifted up the Son of man,
then you will know that I am He
and that I do nothing of my own accord.
But as the Father has taught me, so I speak;
he who sent me is with me,
and has not left me to myself, for I always do what pleases him.'
As he was saying these things, many came to believe in him.

JESUS' ENCOUNTER AT THE Feast of Tabernacles continues. The repeated use of the phrase 'I am He' by Jesus is understood to allude to the name of God revealed to Moses (Exodus 3). As God is, so Jesus is. No wonder there is consternation among Jesus' interlocutors. Jesus furthermore alludes to the healing with the bronze serpent by speaking of himself being 'lifted up'. There is a developing understanding of Jesus, of his relationship with the Father, and of his mission, to be discovered in these chapters of John's gospel. The passage concludes with the statement that 'many came to believe in him', and Jesus will address them.

Jesus is lifted up in death, and in resurrection.
Pray for those who are seeking to know and love Jesus.

WEDNESDAY OF THE FIFTH WEEK IN LENT

A reading from the prophet Daniel (3:14-20, 24-25, 28)

Nebuchadnezzar addressed them, 'Shadrach, Meshach and Abed-Nego, is it true that you do not serve my gods and that you refuse to worship the golden statue I have set up? When you hear the sound of horn, pipe, lyre, zither, harp, bagpipe and every other kind of instrument, are you prepared to prostrate yourselves and worship the statue I have made? If you refuse to worship it, you shall immediately be thrown into the burning fiery furnace; and which of the gods will then save you from my power?' Shadrach, Meshach and Abed-Nego replied to King Nebuchadnezzar, 'Your question needs no answer from us: if our God, whom we serve, is able to save us from the burning fiery furnace and from your power, Your Majesty, he will save us; and even if he does not, then you must know, Your Majesty, that we will not serve your god or worship the statue you have set up.'

This infuriated King Nebuchadnezzar and his face was distorted as he looked at Shadrach, Meshach and Abed-Nego. He gave orders for the furnace to be made seven times hotter than usual and commanded the very strongest men of his army to bind Shadrach, Meshach and Abed-Nego and throw them into the burning fiery furnace.

Then King Nebuchadnezzar sprang to his feet in amazement. He said to his advisers, 'Did we not have these three men thrown bound into the fire?' They answered the king, 'Yes, indeed, Your Majesty.' He replied, 'But I can see four men walking free in the heart of the fire and quite unharmed! And the fourth looks like a child of the gods!'

Nebuchadnezzar said, 'Blessed be the God of Shadrach, Meshach and Abed-Nego: he has sent his angel to rescue his servants who, putting their trust in him, defied the order of the king and preferred to forfeit their bodies rather than serve or worship any god but their God.'

THE THREE YOUNG HEBREWS, Hananiah, Mishael and Azariah, now known by their Babylonian names, have refused to worship Nebuchadnezzar's gods, or the golden statue he has set up. The first chapter of the book of Daniel listed Daniel himself with these three young men when they first arrived in Babylon and began training for service at the court. The miraculous escape of Shadrach, Meshach and Abed-Nego from the furnace provokes the king's change of heart as he exclaims: 'Blessed be the God of Shadrach, Meshach and Abed-Nego.' The story of their escape from the fiery furnace demonstrates the protection afforded by God to his people living under pagan oppression. The God of Israel, being infinitely superior to the gods of the pagans, is able to convince even the worst of tyrants. God provides the strength and salvation needed by those who are persecuted for their faith.

> **Psalm:** The canticle of the three young men is from the Greek Bible and has been inserted into Daniel chapter 3 at this point.

A reading from the holy gospel according to John (8:31-42)

To the Jews who believed in him Jesus said:
'If you remain in my word,
you are truly my disciples;
you will come to know the truth,
and the truth will set you free.'
They answered, 'We are descended from Abraham and we have never been the slaves of anyone; what do you mean, "You will become free?"' Jesus replied:
'Amen, Amen I say to you,
everyone who commits sin is a slave of sin.
Now a slave does not remain in the household for ever,
but a son remains for ever.
So if the Son sets you free,
you will indeed be free.
I know that you are descended from Abraham;
but you seek to kill me
because my word finds no place in you.
I speak of what I have seen at my Father's side,
and you too do what you have learnt from your father.'
They replied to him, 'Our father is Abraham.' Jesus said to them:

'If you were Abraham's children,
you would do as Abraham did.
As it is, you want to kill me,
a man who has told you the truth
which I have learnt from God.
That is not what Abraham did.
You are doing your father's work.'
They replied, 'We were not born illegitimate, the only father we have is God.' Jesus answered:
'If God were your father, you would love me,
since I have my origin in God and have come from him;
I did not come of my own accord,
but he sent me.'

THE EVANGELIST CONTINUES TO present the conversation of Jesus in Jerusalem at the Feast of Tabernacles. Many have come to believe in Jesus, but the mood changes when he suggests that they will be 'set free' by the truth he brings them. They resent the insinuation that they are not already free. Their adherence to Abraham is sufficient, they imply, but their lack of freedom means they refuse to recognise God's word in Jesus. Can they really claim to be children of Abraham, who himself was led by God? Can they really claim to be children of God, if they do not recognise that Jesus has come from the Father?

The road of faith offers new twists and turns, and new surprises. Pray for freedom from rigidity.

THURSDAY OF THE FIFTH WEEK IN LENT

A reading from the book of Genesis (17:3-9)

Abram bowed to the ground. God spoke to him as follows, 'For my part, this is my covenant with you: you will become the father of many nations. And you are no longer to be called Abram; your name is Abraham, for I have made you father of many nations. I shall make you very fertile. I shall make you into nations, and kings will issue from you. And I shall maintain my covenant between myself and you, and your descendants after you, generation after generation, as an everlasting covenant, to be your God and the God of your descendants after you. And to you and to your descendants after you, I give the country where you are now immigrants, the entire land of Canaan, to own in perpetuity. And I will be their God.'

And God said to Abraham, 'You for your part must keep my covenant, you and your descendants after you, generation after generation.'

THE COVENANT (*BERIT*) WITH Abram was first reported in Genesis 15. In this reading, from a later text, the covenant is reiterated, and Abram's change of name to 'Abraham' is announced. The new name, 'Abraham', is traditionally interpreted to mean 'father of a multitude'. The covenant sets up a relationship in which God is the giver and Abraham the receiver. The repeated promise of God is of numerous descendants and of land. In the following verses it will be laid down that all males should undergo circumcision as the 'sign of the covenant' (17:11).

> **Psalm 105 (104)** The psalm refers to the three patriarchs of the covenant, Abraham, Isaac and Jacob.

A reading from the holy gospel according to John (8:51-59)

Jesus said to the Jews:

'Amen, Amen I say to you,
whoever keeps my word will never see death.'

The Jews said, 'Now we know that you have a demon. Abraham died, and the prophets too, and yet you say, "Whoever keeps my word will never taste death." Are you greater than our father Abraham, who died? The prophets died too. Who do you claim to be?'

Jesus answered: 'If I were to seek my own glory
my glory would be worth nothing;
in fact, my glory is conferred by the Father,
by the one of whom you say, "He is our God,"
although you do not know him.

But I know him, and if I were to say,
"I do not know him,"
I should be a liar, like you.
But I do know him, and I keep his word.
Your father Abraham rejoiced
that he should see my day;
he saw it and was glad.'
Then the Jews said, 'You are not yet fifty years old, and you have seen Abraham!' Jesus replied:
'Amen, Amen I say to you,
before Abraham ever was,
I am.'
And they picked up stones to throw at him; but Jesus hid himself and left the Temple.

THE QUESTION RAISED IN THIS continuing dispute at the Feast of Tabernacles is the relationship of Jesus to Abraham. The Jews ask Jesus directly whether he is 'greater than Abraham'. His response leads to the claim that Abraham 'rejoiced to see my day', and the climax comes with Jesus' words: 'before Abraham ever was, I am'. Jesus attributes to Abraham a unique vision of the whole history of salvation. As earlier in the chapter Jesus uses the words 'I am', but here in an absolute sense, echoing the words of God to Moses in Exodus 3. The Jews are outraged and begin to stone him for what they consider to be blasphemy (10:33). When there is no faith insults are an easy way out.

How could Abraham rejoice to see the day of Christ?
Let us pray for those who cannot open their eyes to new vision.

FRIDAY OF THE FIFTH WEEK IN LENT

A reading from the prophet Jeremiah (20:10-13)

Jeremiah said:
'I heard so many whispering about me,

"Terror on every side!
Denounce him! Let us denounce him!"
All those who seemed at peace with me
were watching for me to slip,
"Perhaps he will be tricked into error.
Then we shall get the better of him
and then we can take our revenge!"
But the LORD is at my side like a mighty hero.
So my opponents will stumble
and will not prevail.
Utterly shamed by their failure,
their eternal disgrace will not be forgotten.
LORD Sabaoth, you who test the righteous,
you see the heart and the mind;
I shall see your vengeance on them,
for I have revealed my cause to you.
Sing to the LORD, praise the LORD,
for he delivers the life of the needy
from the hands of evildoers.'

THINGS GROW EVER MORE desperate in the prophetic ministry of Jeremiah, who has to warn his people in the face of the approaching catastrophe of Babylonian aggression. Plots against him for his supposed disloyalty lead to this most anguished of his confessions. He reports the words of his enemies: 'Terror on every side! Denounce him!' They plot their revenge against the prophet. Jeremiah pleads for God to intervene, and in his extreme situation asks for vengeance. He maintains his confidence in the Lord, who 'is like a mighty hero' and 'delivers the life of the needy from the hands of evildoers'.

> **Psalm 18 (17)** The psalm expresses similar anguish as 'waves of death' threaten to overwhelm, but God 'hears the voice' of the one who prays.

FIFTH WEEK IN LENT

A reading from the holy gospel according to John (10:31-42)

The Jews again took up stones to stone him, so Jesus said to them, 'I have shown you many good works from my Father. For which of these are you stoning me?' The Jews answered him, 'We are stoning you, not for doing a good work, but for blasphemy; though you are only a man, you are making yourself God.' Jesus answered:

'Is it not written in your Law:
I said, you are gods?
If it uses the word "gods"
of those people to whom the word of God was addressed
and scripture cannot be annulled –
can you say of someone whom the Father has consecrated
and sent into the world, "You are blaspheming",
because I said, "I am Son of God"?
If I am not doing my Father's work,
do not believe me.
But if I am doing it,
then even if you do not believe me,
at least believe the works I do;
so that you know and recognise
that the Father is in me and I am in the Father.'

They again sought to arrest him, but he escaped from their hands.

He went back again to the far side of the Jordan, to the district where John had first been baptising, and he stayed there. Many people who came to him said, 'John gave no signs, but all he said about this man was true'; and many there believed in him.

THIS EXCERPT FROM JOHN chapter 10 sees Jesus in Jerusalem for the Feast of Dedication. It seems that his statement in 10:30 'The Father and I are one' provoked this further attempt to stone Jesus, which reflects the growing antagonism and violence of his opponents. Jesus uses Scripture to demonstrate that his claims are not offensive to the Father. As earlier, in the discussion after the healing of the paralysed man in John 5, Jesus speaks of the 'works' which he performs as proving that he is from the Father. Things grow more dangerous for Jesus, but for now he escapes arrest. His refuge on the far side of the Jordan, where John had baptised, is a return to the place where his ministry began. Is Jesus renewing his strength for what lies ahead? This is also a place where there is faith, for 'many there believed in him.'

Be encouraged by the faith of those around you, even if it is hidden. Pray for those who believe despite rejection and persecution.

SATURDAY OF THE FIFTH WEEK IN LENT

A reading from the prophet Ezekiel (37:21-28)

Thus says the Lord GOD: 'Look, I am taking the Israelites from the nations where they have gone. I shall gather them together from everywhere and bring them home to their own soil. I shall make them into one nation in the country, on the mountains of Israel, and one king is to be king of them all; they will no longer form two nations, nor be two separate kingdoms. They will no longer defile themselves with their idols, their horrors and any of their crimes. I shall save them from the acts of infidelity which they have committed and I shall cleanse them; they will be my people and I shall be their God. My servant David will reign over them, one shepherd for all; they will follow my judgements, respect my laws and practise them. They will live in the land which I gave to my servant Jacob, the land in which your ancestors lived. They will live in it, they, their children, their children's children, for ever. David my servant is to be their prince for ever. I shall make a covenant of peace with them, an eternal covenant with them. I shall resettle them and make them grow; I shall set my sanctuary among them for ever. I shall make my home above them; I shall be their God and they will be my people. And the nations will know that I am the LORD, the sanctifier of Israel, when my sanctuary is with them for evermore.'

IN HIS WORDS OF promise about the future, after the return from exile, the prophet Ezekiel speaks of a reunited people. Many centuries earlier, after the death of king Solomon, the kingdom of David had split into the northern kingdom of Israel and the southern kingdom of Judah (1 Kings 12). God now instructs Ezekiel to perform the symbolic act of bringing together two sticks to symbolise reunion (37:15-20). The two nations shall become one, under one ruler, and the covenant shall be restored, an 'eternal covenant of peace'. It is twice stated that 'David' will rule over them, for David was the ideal king in a time of unity. The sanctuary of God shall be among them for ever. God proclaims: 'I shall be their God, and they will be my people.' The nations will know by this the greatness of the God of Israel.

> **Jer 31:10-31** In this prophetic poem Jeremiah looks forward to a time of consolation.

A reading from the holy gospel according to John (11:45-56)

Many of the Jews who had come to visit Mary, and had seen what he did, believed in him, but some of them went to the Pharisees to tell them what Jesus had done. Then the chief priests and Pharisees called a meeting and said, 'What are we doing? This man is working many signs. If we let him go on in this way everybody will believe in him, and the Romans will come and take from us the Holy Place and our nation.' One of them, Caiaphas, who was high priest that year, said, 'You know nothing at all; you have not worked out that it is better for you that one man should die for the people, rather than that the whole nation should perish.' He did not speak in his own person, but as high priest of that year he was prophesying that Jesus was to die for the nation – and not for the nation only, but also to gather together into one the dispersed children of God. From that day onwards they planned to kill him. So Jesus no longer went about openly among the Jews, but left there for the district near the desert, to a town called Ephraim, and stayed there with the disciples.

The Passover of the Jews was near, and many people came up from the country to Jerusalem before the Passover to purify themselves. They were looking out for Jesus, saying to one another as they stood in the Temple, 'What do you think? Surely he will not come to the festival, will he?'

READING THE BIBLE THROUGH LENT

AFTER THE FINAL 'SIGN' of Jesus, the raising of Lazarus from the dead, many more come to believe in him. But others report the event, and the chief priests and Pharisees consider the way forward. The high priest, who was both the religious and political leader, reasons that the death of an innocent man, Jesus, is justified in order to protect the people against Roman repression. To allow this 'messiah' to continue would be to invite further Roman violence against the people. The evangelist considers the statement of Caiaphas to be prophetic, for Jesus will indeed die not only 'for the people', but 'to gather together the dispersed children of God'. The authorities will eventually plot to kill not only Jesus, but Lazarus too (12:10). The evangelist once again reports that Jesus withdraws, this time to the desert and to 'a town called Ephraim'. The last gospel reading before Holy Week begins leaves us in suspense. Will Jesus come to Jerusalem for the feast of Passover? Or will he avoid such a dangerous situation? For their part, the leaders are resolved to have him killed.

Why does leadership so often disregard justice and truth?
We pray that politicians will enlist the power of truth and of justice.

HOLY WEEK

PALM SUNDAY OF THE PASSION OF THE LORD – YEAR A

Before the procession the Gospel of the Entry into Jerusalem is read from Matthew 21:1-11.

A reading from the prophet Isaiah (50:4-7)
The Lord God has given me a disciple's tongue,
to know how to comfort the weary with a word.
Morning by morning he sharpens my ear
to listen like a disciple.
The Lord God has opened my ear
and I did not rebel or turn away.
I offered my back to those who struck me,
my cheeks to those who plucked my beard;
I did not turn away my face from insult and spitting.
The Lord God comes to my help:
therefore no insult has touched me,
therefore I have set my face like flint.
I know that I shall not be shamed.

THE SECTION OF THE Book of Isaiah known as 'Second Isaiah' (Isaiah 40-55) contains four poems probably from the exilic period which are known as the Songs of the Servant. All four are proclaimed during Holy Week, the last and longest on Good Friday, for they are understood by Christians as foreshadowing the sufferings of Christ. Today we hear the third of these songs, in which the Servant is subjected to abuse for speaking words of comfort. The subjection to 'insult and spitting' is reminiscent of the treatment of Jesus during the night before he died. But the Servant knows he shall not 'be shamed'.

> **Psalm 22 (21)** The psalm has many connections with the story of the Passion. The suffering man cries out to God, and the passers-by deride him.

A reading from the letter of St Paul to the Philippians (2:6-11)

Christ Jesus, being in the form of God,
did not count equality with God
something to be grasped.
But he emptied himself,
taking the form of a slave,
born in human likeness,
and found in human shape;
he humbled himself,
becoming obedient unto death, death on a cross.
And therefore God highly exalted him,
and granted him the name above every name
so that at the name of Jesus
every knee should bend
of beings heavenly, earthly and under the earth,
and *every tongue acknowledge*
that Jesus Christ is Lord,
to the glory of God the Father.

THIS CHRISTIAN HYMN WAS probably inserted by St Paul in his letter to the people of Philippi, a community for whom he had a high regard and great affection. The hymn explains the paschal mystery of the humiliation and death of Christ and his being raised up by God. The hymn claims divine status for Jesus for 'every knee shall bend' and Jesus shall be declared 'Lord'. All this is 'to the glory of God the Father'.

The Passion of our Lord Jesus Christ according to Matthew (26:14 – 27:66)

Then one of the Twelve, the man called Judas Iscariot, went to the chief priests and said, 'What are you prepared to give me if I hand him over to you?' They settled with him for thirty silver pieces, and from then onwards he began to look for an opportunity to betray him.

Now on the first day of Unleavened Bread the disciples came to Jesus to say, 'Where do you want us to make the preparations for you to eat the Passover?' He said, 'Go to a certain man in the city and say to him, "The teacher says: My time is near. It is at your house that I am keeping Passover with my disciples."' The disciples did what Jesus told them and prepared the Passover. When evening came he was at table with the Twelve. And while they were eating he said, 'Amen I say to you, one of you is about to betray me.' They were greatly distressed and started asking him in turn, 'Not me, Lord, surely?' He answered, 'Someone who has dipped his hand into the dish with me will betray me. The Son of man is going to his fate, as it is written about him, but alas for that man by whom the Son of man is betrayed! It would have been better for that man if he had never been born!' Judas, who was to betray him, asked in his turn, 'Not me, Rabbi, surely?' Jesus answered, 'It is you who said it.'

Now as they were eating, Jesus took bread, and when he had said the blessing he broke it and giving it to the disciples he said, 'Take it and eat, this is my body.' Then taking a cup, after giving thanks he handed it to them saying, 'Drink from this, all of you, for this is my blood, the blood of the covenant, poured out for many for the forgiveness of sins. From now on, I tell you, I shall never again drink wine until the day I drink the new wine with you in the kingdom of my Father.'

Having sung the psalms they left for the Mount of Olives. Then Jesus said to them, 'You will all fall away from me tonight, for it is written, *I shall strike the shepherd and the sheep of the flock will be scattered*, but after I have been raised up I shall go before you into Galilee.' At this, Peter said to him, 'Even if all fall away from you, I will never fall away.' Jesus answered him, 'Amen I say to you, this very night, before the cock crows, you will deny me three times.' Peter said to him, 'Even if I have to die with you, I will never deny you.' And all the disciples spoke similarly.

Then Jesus came with them to a plot of land called Gethsemane; and he said to his disciples, 'Sit here while I go over there to pray.' He took Peter and the two sons of Zebedee with him. And he began to feel sadness and anguish. Then he said to them, 'My soul is sorrowful to the point of death. Wait here and stay awake with me.' And going on a little further he fell on his face and prayed, saying, 'My Father, if it is possible, let this cup pass from me. Only not as I want, but as you.'

He came back to the disciples and found them sleeping, and he said to Peter, 'So you had not the strength to stay awake with me for one hour? Stay awake, and pray not to enter into temptation. The spirit is eager, but the flesh is weak.' Again, a second time, he went away and prayed, saying, 'My Father, if this cup cannot pass by unless I drink it, your will be done!' And he came back again and found them sleeping, for their eyes were weighed down. Leaving them there, he went away again and prayed for the third time, repeating the same words. Then he came back to the disciples and said to them, 'Sleep on now and have your rest. Look, the hour is near when the Son of man is betrayed into the hands of sinners. Get up! Let us go! Look, my betrayer is near.'

And suddenly, while he was still speaking, Judas, one of the Twelve, came, and with him a large crowd armed with swords and clubs, sent by the chief priests and elders of the people. Now the traitor had given them a sign, saying, 'The one I kiss, he is the man. Take charge of him.' So he went up to Jesus at once and said, 'Greetings, Rabbi,' and kissed him. Jesus said to him, 'My friend, do what you are here for.' Then they came forward, laid hands on Jesus and took charge of him. And suddenly, one of the followers of Jesus grasped his sword and drew it; he struck the high priest's servant and cut off his ear. Then Jesus said, 'Put your sword back into its place, for all who draw the sword will die by the sword. Or do you think that I cannot appeal to my Father, who would promptly send more than twelve legions of angels to my defence? But then, how would the scriptures be fulfilled, which say that it must happen this way?' At that hour Jesus said to the crowds, 'Have you come out with swords and clubs to capture me as though I were a bandit? Day by day I sat teaching in the Temple and you did not lay hands on me.' Now all this happened so that the scriptures of the prophets should be fulfilled. Then all the disciples deserted him and ran away.

The men who had arrested Jesus led him off to Caiaphas the high priest, where the scribes and the elders were assembled. Peter followed him at a distance right to the courtyard of the high priest, and he went inside and sat down with the attendants to see what the end would be.

The chief priests and the whole council were looking for false evidence against Jesus, on which they might have him executed. But they could not find any, though many false witnesses came forward. Eventually two came forward and said, 'This man said, "I have power to destroy the Temple of God and in three days build it up."' Then the high priest rose and said to him, 'Have you no answer to the evidence these men are bringing against you?' But Jesus was silent. And the high priest said to him, 'I put you on oath by the living God to tell us if you are the Messiah, the Son of God.' Jesus answered him, 'It is you who say it. Only, I tell you that from this time onward you will see *the Son of man seated at the right hand of the Power and coming on the clouds of heaven*.' Then the high priest tore his clothes and said, 'He has blasphemed. Why do we still need witnesses? See now! You have heard the blasphemy. What do you think?' They said in answer, 'He deserves to die.' Then they spat in his face and hit him with their fists, saying, 'Prophesy to us, Messiah! Who hit you?'

Meanwhile Peter was sitting outside in the courtyard, and a servant-girl came up to him saying, 'You, too, were with Jesus the Galilean.' But he denied it in front of them all, saying, 'I do not know or understand what you mean.' When he went out into the gateway another servant-girl saw him and said to the people there, 'This man was with Jesus the Nazarene.' And again, with an oath, he denied it, 'I do not know the man.' A little later the bystanders came up and said to Peter, 'You are certainly one of them too! Why, your accent gives you away.' Then he started cursing and swearing, 'I do not know the man.' And at once the cock crowed, and Peter remembered what Jesus had said, 'Before the cock crows you will deny me three times.' And he went outside and wept bitterly.

When morning came, all the chief priests and the elders of the people met in council to bring about the death of Jesus. They bound him, took him off and handed him over to Pilate, the governor.

When Judas, his betrayer, saw that Jesus had been condemned, he was filled with remorse and took the thirty silver pieces back to the chief priests and elders, saying, 'I have sinned by betraying innocent blood.' They replied, 'What is that to us? See to it yourself.' And flinging down the silver pieces in the sanctuary he made off, and went and hanged himself. The chief priests picked up the silver pieces and said, 'It is not permissible to put this into the treasury; since it is blood-money.' So they discussed the matter and with it bought the potter's field as a graveyard for foreigners, and this is why the field has been called the Field of Blood till this day. The word spoken through the prophet Jeremiah was then fulfilled: *And they took the thirty silver pieces, the sum at which the precious One was priced by the children of Israel, and they gave them for the potter's field, just as the Lord directed me.*

Jesus, then, was brought before the governor, and the governor put to him this question, 'Are you the king of the Jews?' Jesus replied, 'You say so.' But when he was accused by the chief priests and the elders he did not answer. Pilate then said to him, 'Do you not hear how many accusations they are bringing against you?' But he did not answer a single word to him, so that the governor was amazed.

At festival time it was the governor's practice to release a prisoner for the people, anyone they chose. Now they had then a notorious prisoner called Barabbas. So when they had gathered, Pilate said to them, 'Which do you want me to release for you, Barabbas, or Jesus who is called the Messiah?' For Pilate knew it was out of jealousy that they had handed him over.

Now as he was seated in the chair of judgement, his wife sent him a message, 'Have nothing to do with that righteous man; I have been extremely upset today by a dream that I had about him.' The chief priests and the elders, however, had persuaded the crowds to ask for the release of Barabbas and the execution of Jesus. So when the governor spoke and asked them, 'Which of the two do you want me to release for you?' they said, 'Barabbas.' Pilate said to them, 'What, then, am I to do with Jesus who is called the Messiah?' They all said, 'Let him be crucified!' He asked, 'What evil has he done?' But they shouted all the more, 'Let him be crucified!' Then Pilate, seeing that he was making no impression, but rather that a riot was imminent, took some water, washed his hands in front of the crowd and said, 'I am innocent of this man's blood. You see to it.' And the whole people shouted back, 'Let his blood be on us and on our children!' Then he released Barabbas for them. After having Jesus scourged, he handed him over to be crucified.

Then the governor's soldiers took Jesus with them into the Praetorium and collected the whole cohort round him. And they stripped him and put a scarlet cloak round him, and having twisted some thorns into a crown they put this on his head and placed a reed in his right hand. To make fun of him they knelt to him saying, 'Hail, king of the Jews!' And they spat at him and took the reed and struck him on the head. And when they had mocked him, they took off the cloak and dressed him in his own clothes and led him away to crucifixion.

On their way out, they came across a man from Cyrene, called Simon, and enlisted him to carry his cross. When they had reached a place called Golgotha, which is called the place of the skull, they gave him wine to drink mixed with gall, which he tasted but refused to drink. When they had crucified him they shared out his clothing by casting lots, and then, sitting down, they guarded him there. And they placed above his head the charge against him; it read: 'This is Jesus, the King of the Jews.' Then they crucified two bandits with him, one on his right and one on his left. The passers-by jeered at him, shaking their heads and saying, 'You who destroy the Temple and in three days rebuild it, save yourself, if you are God's son, and come down from the cross!' The chief priests with the scribes and elders mocked him in the same way, with the words, 'He saved others; he cannot save himself. He is the king of Israel; let him come down from the cross now, and we will believe in him. He has put his trust in God; now let God rescue him if he wants him. For he said, "I am God's son."' In the same way even the bandits who were crucified with him taunted him.

From noon onwards there was darkness over all the land until mid-afternoon. And at that time, Jesus cried out in a loud voice, '*Eli, eli, lama sabachthani?*' that is, '*My God, my God, why have you forsaken me?*' When some of the bystanders there heard this, they said, 'He is calling on Elijah,' and one of them at once ran to get a sponge which he filled with vinegar and, putting it on a reed, gave it him to drink. But the rest of them said, 'Wait! Let us see if Elijah comes to save him.' But Jesus, again crying out in a loud voice, yielded up his spirit.

And suddenly, the veil of the sanctuary was torn in two from top to bottom, the earth quaked, the rocks were split, the tombs opened and the bodies of many holy people rose from the dead, and these, after his resurrection, came out of the tombs, entered the holy city and appeared to a number of people. The centurion, together with the others guarding Jesus, had seen the earthquake and all that was taking place, and they were terrified and said, 'In truth this man was son of God.'

And many women were there, watching from a distance, the same women who had followed Jesus from Galilee and looked after him. Among them were Mary of Magdala, Mary the mother of James and Joseph, and the mother of Zebedee's sons.

When it was evening, there came a rich man of Arimathaea, called Joseph, who had himself become a disciple of Jesus. This man went to Pilate and asked for the body of Jesus. Then Pilate ordered it to be handed over. So Joseph took the body, wrapped it in a clean linen cloth, and put it in his own new tomb which he had hewn in the rock. Then he rolled a large stone to the doorway of the tomb and went away. Now Mary of Magdala and the other Mary were there, sitting opposite the sepulchre. Next day, that is, when Preparation Day was over, the chief priests and the Pharisees gathered before Pilate and said to him, 'Sir, we recall that this deceiver said, while he was still alive, "After three days I shall rise again." Therefore give the order to have the sepulchre kept secure until the third day, for fear his disciples come and steal him away and tell the people, "He has been raised from the dead." This last fraud would be worse than the first.' Pilate said to them, 'You have a guard; go and make all as secure as you know how.' So they went and made the sepulchre secure, putting seals on the stone with the guard.

EACH GOSPEL NARRATIVE OF the passion and death of Jesus has its own particularities, for each evangelist seeks to emphasise different aspects of the story. Our narrative from Matthew begins with Judas' betrayal, and this evangelist alone gives the detail of 'thirty silver pieces', thus indicating with a reference from the prophet Zechariah (11:12) the paltry sum at which the Messiah was valued. Matthew emphasises the tragic role of Judas, and alone reports his words at the supper 'Not me, Rabbi, surely?' Jesus poignantly addresses Judas as 'friend' when he comes with the arresting party to Gethsemane, and Matthew will end the story of Judas with the detail of his despair and suicide. Matthew seems to have a particular interest in Pontius Pilate too. Pilate's wife, a Gentile, warns Pilate to have nothing to do with 'that righteous man', but Pilate simply 'washed his hands' of Jesus, allowing the crowds to have their way. Only in this gospel do we hear the fearful cry 'Let his blood be on us and on our children!' The events after the death of Jesus are particularly significant in this gospel. The earth quakes and the rocks split and the saints rise from their tombs to be seen by many in the holy city. The Roman centurion, a pagan, and 'the others guarding Jesus' assert with one voice their faith in his identity: 'In truth this man was son of God.' While on the one hand Matthew stresses the people's guilt for the death of Jesus, he also suggests that pagans are drawn to him in faith.

Matthew shows that, while the religious leaders plot against Jesus, the Gentiles are open to his mystery.
Pray for harmonious relations between Jewish and Christian believers.

PALM SUNDAY OF THE PASSION OF THE LORD – YEAR B

Before the procession the Gospel of the Entry into Jerusalem is read from Mark 11:1-10.
The first reading, responsorial psalm and second reading are from Year A.

The Passion of our Lord Jesus Christ according to Mark (14:1 – 15:47)

It was two days before the Passover and the feast of Unleavened Bread, and the chief priests and the scribes were looking for a way to arrest Jesus by some trick and kill him. For they said, 'Not during the feast, or there may be a disturbance among the people.'

When he was at Bethany in the house of Simon the leper, while he was at table a woman came in with an alabaster jar of very costly ointment, pure nard. She broke the jar and poured the ointment on his head. There were some who said to one another indignantly, 'Why has this waste of ointment happened? This ointment could have been sold for over three hundred denarii and the money given to the poor'; and they were angry with her. But Jesus said, 'Leave her alone. Why are you upsetting her? She has done me a good service. You have the poor with you always, and you can benefit them whenever you wish, but me you will not always have. She has done what she could: she has anointed my body beforehand for its burial. Amen I say to you, wherever throughout all the world the gospel is proclaimed, what she has done will also be told, in remembrance of her.'

Judas Iscariot, one of the Twelve, went off to the chief priests so that he might hand Jesus over to them. Hearing it, they were delighted, and promised to give him money; and he began to look for a way of betraying him at an opportune time.

On the first day of Unleavened Bread, when they used to sacrifice the Passover lamb, his disciples said to him, 'Where do you want us to go and make the preparations for you to eat the Passover?' So he sent two of his disciples, saying to them, 'Go into the city and someone will meet you carrying a pitcher of water. Follow him, and wherever he enters say to the owner of the house, "The teacher says: Where is the room where I may eat the Passover with my disciples?" He will show you a large upper room ready set out. Make the preparations for us there.' The disciples set out and went to the city and found everything as he had told them, and prepared the Passover.

When evening came he arrived with the Twelve. And while they were at table eating, Jesus said, 'Amen I say to you, one of you is about to betray me, one of you *eating with me*.' They were distressed and said to him, one after another, 'Not me, surely?' He said to them, 'It is one of the Twelve, one who is dipping into the same dish with me. For the Son of man is going to his fate, as it is written about him, but alas for that man by whom the Son of man is betrayed! Better for that man if he had never been born.'

And as they were eating he took bread, and when he had said the blessing he broke it, gave it to them and said, 'Take it, this is my body.' Then taking a cup, after giving thanks he gave it to them, and all drank from it, and he said to them, 'This is my blood of the covenant, poured out for many. Amen I say to you, I shall never again drink wine until that day when I drink new wine in the kingdom of God.'

Having sung the psalms they left for the Mount of Olives. And Jesus said to them, 'You will all fall away, for it is written: *I shall strike the shepherd and the sheep will be scattered*; however, after I have been raised up I shall go before you into Galilee.' Peter said, 'Even if all fall away, I will not.' And Jesus said to him, 'Amen I say to you, today, this very night, before the cock crows twice, you will deny me three times.' But he repeated still more strongly, 'Even if I have to die with you, I will never deny you.' And they all said the same.

HOLY WEEK

They came to a plot of land called Gethsemane, and he said to his disciples, 'Sit here while I pray.' Then he took Peter and James and John with him. And he began to feel dismay and anguish. And he said to them, 'My soul is deeply sorrowful to the point of death. Wait here, and stay awake.' And going on a little further he began falling to the ground and prayed that, if it were possible, this hour might pass away from him. And he said, '*Abba*, Father! For you everything is possible. Take this cup away from me. Yet not what I want but what you want.' He came and found them sleeping, and he said to Peter, 'Simon, are you asleep? Had you not the strength to stay awake one hour? Stay awake and pray not to enter into temptation. The spirit is eager, but flesh is weak.' Again he went away and prayed, saying the same words. And once more he came and found them sleeping, for their eyes were weighed down; and they did not know how they should answer him. He came a third time and said to them, 'Sleep on and have your rest. Enough! The hour has come. See, the Son of man is being betrayed into the hands of sinners. Get up! Let us go! See, my betrayer is not far away.'

And at once, while he was still speaking, Judas, one of the Twelve, came up, and with him a crowd with swords and clubs from the chief priests and the scribes and the elders. Now the traitor had arranged a sign with them saying, 'The one I will kiss, he is the man. Take charge of him, and lead him away securely.' So when he came, he went up to Jesus at once and said, 'Rabbi!' and kissed him. The others laid hands on him and took charge of him. Then one of the bystanders drew his sword and struck out at the high priest's servant and cut off his ear.

Then Jesus replied saying, 'Have you come out with swords and clubs to capture me as though I were a bandit? Day by day I was among you teaching in the Temple and you did not lay hands on me. But let the scriptures be fulfilled.' And they all deserted him and fled. A young man was following him with nothing on but a linen cloth. They caught hold of him, but he left the cloth behind and fled naked.

They led Jesus off to the high priest; and all the chief priests and the elders and the scribes assembled. Peter had followed him at a distance, right into the courtyard of the high priest, and was sitting with the attendants warming himself at the fire.

The chief priests and the whole council were looking for evidence against Jesus in order to put him to death. But they could not find any, for many gave false evidence against him, but their evidence did not agree. Some stood up and gave this false evidence against him, 'We heard him say, "I will destroy this Temple made by human hands, and in three days build another, not made by human hands."' But even so their evidence did not agree. The high priest then stood up before the whole council and questioned Jesus saying, 'Have you no answer at all to the evidence they are bringing against you?' But he was silent and made no answer at all. Again the high priest questioned him saying, 'Are you the Messiah, the Son of the Blessed One?' Jesus said, 'I am; and you will see the *Son of man seated at the right hand of the Power and coming with the clouds of heaven.*' Then the high priest tore his clothes and said, 'Why do we still need witnesses? You heard the blasphemy. What is your opinion?' They all condemned him as deserving death.

Some of them started to spit at him, cover his face, buffet him and say 'Prophesy!' And the attendants took him over, slapping him in the face.

While Peter was down below in the courtyard, one of the high priest's servant-girls came up. She saw Peter warming himself there, she stared at him and said, 'You were with Jesus, the man from Nazareth, too.' But he denied it saying, 'I do not know, and do not understand what you are talking about.' And he went out into the forecourt, and a cock crowed. And seeing him the servant-girl again started saying to the bystanders, 'This man is one of them.' But again he denied it. A little later the bystanders themselves said to Peter, 'You certainly are one of them! You are a Galilean too.' But he started cursing and swearing, 'I do not know this man you are talking about.' And at once the cock crowed for the second time, and Peter recalled how Jesus had said to him, 'Before the cock crows twice, you will deny me three times.' And he burst into tears.

And at once in the morning, the chief priests, together with the elders and scribes and the rest of the assembly, having prepared a plan and bound Jesus, took him off and handed him over to Pilate. Pilate asked him, 'Are you the king of the Jews?' He replied, 'You say so.' And the chief priests brought many accusations against him. Pilate questioned him again, 'Do you make no reply at all? See how many accusations they are bringing against you!' But Jesus made no further reply, so that Pilate was amazed.

HOLY WEEK

At festival time Pilate used to release a prisoner for them, any one they asked for. Now someone called Barabbas was then in prison with the rebels who had committed murder during the uprising. When the crowd went up and began to ask Pilate to do the customary favour for them, Pilate answered them, 'Do you want me to release for you the king of the Jews?' For he realised it was out of spite that the chief priests had handed Jesus over. The chief priests, however, stirred up the crowd so that he should release Barabbas for them instead. Then Pilate spoke to them again, 'What, then, am I to do with the man you call king of the Jews?' They shouted back, 'Crucify him!' Pilate asked them, 'What evil has he done?' But they shouted all the more, 'Crucify him!' So Pilate, anxious to satisfy the crowd, released Barabbas for them and, after having Jesus scourged, handed him over to be crucified.

The soldiers led him away to the inner part of the palace, that is, the Praetorium, and called the whole cohort together. They clothed him in purple, twisted some thorns into a crown and put it on him. And they began saluting him, 'Hail, king of the Jews!' They struck his head with a reed and spat on him; and kneeling down they worshipped him. And when they had mocked him, they took off the purple, dressed him in his own clothes and led him out to crucify him.

They enlisted a passer-by, Simon of Cyrene, father of Alexander and Rufus, who was coming from the country, to carry his cross. They brought Jesus to the place called Golgotha, which means the place of the skull.

They offered him wine mixed with myrrh, but he did not take it. Then they crucified him, and *shared out his clothes by casting lots* to decide what each should take. It was mid-morning when they crucified him. The inscription of the charge against him read, 'The King of the Jews'. And they crucified two bandits with him, one on his right and one on his left. The passers-by jeered at him, shaking their heads and saying, 'Aha! You who destroy the Temple and rebuild it in three days, save yourself! Come down from the cross!' The chief priests and the scribes mocked him among themselves in the same way saying, 'He saved others, he cannot save himself. Let the Messiah, the king of Israel, come down from the cross now, so that we may see it and believe.' Those who were crucified with him also taunted him.

When noon came there was darkness over the whole land until

mid-afternoon. And at that time Jesus cried out in a loud voice, '*Eloi, eloi, lama sabachthani?*' which means, '*My God, my God, why have you forsaken me?*' When some of the bystanders heard, they said, 'Listen, he is calling Elijah.' And someone ran and soaked a sponge in vinegar and, putting it on a stick, gave it to him to drink saying, 'Wait! Let us see if Elijah comes to take him down.' But Jesus let out a loud cry and breathed his last. And the curtain of the Temple was torn in two from top to bottom. The centurion, who was standing opposite him, seeing that he had breathed his last, said, 'In truth this man was Son of God.'

There were some women watching from a distance. Among them were Mary of Magdala, Mary who was the mother of James the younger and Joset, and Salome. These used to follow him and look after him when he was in Galilee. And many other women were there who had come up to Jerusalem with him.

Now as soon as evening came, since it was Preparation Day – that is, the day before the Sabbath – Joseph of Arimathaea, a respected member of the council, who was himself awaiting the kingdom of God, went boldly to Pilate and asked for the body of Jesus. Pilate, surprised if he was already dead, summoned the centurion and asked if he had been long dead. Having been assured of this by the centurion, he granted the corpse to Joseph. Joseph bought a linen cloth, and taking him down from the cross, wrapped him in the shroud, laid him in a tomb which had been hewn out of the rock and rolled a stone against the doorway of the tomb. Mary of Magdala and Mary the mother of Joset were watching where he was laid.

THE STORY OF THE death of Jesus in the Gospel of Mark is the earliest account. These final chapters of the gospel contain in narrative form what is the essence of Christian preaching: the death and resurrection of Christ. The whole gospel of Mark leads to this climax. Jesus journeys just once to Jerusalem, the place of his martyrdom, and on the way speaks starkly about what he foresees to the shocked disciples. In Gethsemane Mark describes Jesus as feeling 'dismay and anguish', while the disciples sleep. When the crowd arrives to arrest Jesus, the disciples flee, joined by a young man wrapped in a 'linen cloth'. As false accusations are brought against Jesus, Peter equally falsely denies Jesus three times with increasing vehemence. Pilate is amazed at the silence of Jesus. Eventually, in order to 'satisfy the crowd', and for his own political ends, he hands Jesus over to be crucified. The scene described on Golgotha is stark, as Jesus is derided by the passers-by, by the chief priests and scribes, and by both of the two bandits crucified with him. His words from the cross are the poignant beginning of Psalm 22: 'My God, my God, why have you forsaken me?' As in the other synoptic gospels it is the centurion who after his death makes a declaration of faith in Jesus. Mark stresses that at his burial the women 'were watching where he was laid'.

The story of the Passion is the climax of the gospel.
Pray for those who use religion for violence and domination.

PALM SUNDAY OF THE PASSION OF THE LORD – YEAR C

Before the procession the Gospel of the Entry into Jerusalem is read from Luke 19:28-40.
The first reading, responsorial psalm and second reading are from Year A.

The Passion of our Lord Jesus Christ according to Luke (22:14 – 23:56)

When the time came he took his place at table, and the apostles with him. And he said to them, 'I have ardently longed to eat this Passover with you before I suffer; because, I tell you, I shall not eat it until it is fulfilled in the kingdom of God.' Then, taking a cup, he gave thanks and said, 'Take this and share it among you, because from now on, I tell you, I shall never again drink from the fruit of the vine until the kingdom of God comes.'

Then he took bread, and when he had given thanks, he broke it and gave it to them, saying, 'This is my body given for you; do this in remembrance of me.' And the cup similarly after supper saying, 'This cup is the new covenant in my blood, poured out for you.

'But look, here with me on the table is the hand of the man who is betraying me. The Son of man is indeed going as it is decreed, only alas for that man by whom he is betrayed!' And they began to question one another which of them it could be who intended to do this.

An argument also began between them about who of them should be reckoned the greatest; but he said to them, 'The kings of the gentiles lord it over them, and those who have authority over them are given the title Benefactor. Not so with you, but the greatest among you must be as the youngest, the leader as the one who serves. For who is the greater: the one at table or the one who serves? The one at table, surely? Yet I am among you as one who serves!

'You are those who have endured with me in my trials; and now I confer a kingdom on you, just as my Father conferred one on me. You may eat and drink at my table in my kingdom, and you will sit on thrones judging the twelve tribes of Israel.

'Simon, Simon! Look, Satan has been granted to sift you all like wheat; but I have prayed for you, Simon, that your faith may not fail; and sometime you must turn back and strengthen your brothers.' He answered, 'Lord, with you I am ready to go to prison and to death.' Jesus replied, 'I tell you, Peter, the cock will not crow today before you have denied three times that you know me.'

He said to them, 'When I sent you out without purse or bag or sandals, were you short of anything?' They answered, 'Nothing.' He said to them, 'But now anyone who has a purse, should take it, and the same with a bag; anyone who has no sword, should sell his tunic and buy one, for I say to you that this scripture must be fulfilled in me, He was reckoned as one of the lawless. And indeed what is written about me is being fulfilled.' They said, 'Lord, here are two swords.' He said to them, 'That is enough!'

He then left to make his way as usual to the Mount of Olives, with the disciples following. When he reached the place he said to them, 'Pray that you do not enter into temptation.'

Then he withdrew from them, about a stone's throw, and knelt down and prayed, saying, 'Father, if you are willing, take this cup away from me. Yet not my will but yours be done.' Then an angel from heaven appeared to him, strengthening him. In his anguish he prayed more earnestly, and his sweat became like drops of blood falling to the ground.

Standing up from prayer and going to the disciples he found them sleeping from grief.

And he said to them, 'Why are you asleep? Get up and pray that you do not enter into temptation.'

While he was still speaking, a crowd suddenly appeared, and the one called Judas, one of the Twelve, was leading them. And he approached Jesus to kiss him. Jesus said, 'Judas, are you betraying the Son of man with a kiss?' Those around him, seeing what was going to happen, said, 'Lord, shall we strike with the sword?' And one of them struck the high priest's servant and cut off his right ear. But at this Jesus said, 'Leave it at that!' And touching his ear he healed him.

Then Jesus said to the chief priests and officers of the guard and elders who had come for him, 'Have you come with swords and clubs as though I were a bandit? When I was with you in the Temple day by day you did not lift a hand against me. But this is your hour and the reign of darkness.'

They seized him then and led him away, and they took him into the high priest's house. Peter followed at a distance. When they had lit a fire in the middle of the courtyard and had sat down together, Peter sat down among them, and a servant-girl, seeing him sitting in the light, peered at him, and said, 'This man was with him too.' But he denied it saying. 'I do not know him, woman.' Shortly afterwards someone else saw him and said, 'You are one of them too.' But Peter replied, 'Man, I am not.' A little later another person saw him and insisted, 'For certain this man was with him also, for he is a Galilean too.' Peter said, 'Man, I do not know what you are talking about.' And immediately, while he was still speaking, the cock crowed, and the Lord turned and looked straight at Peter, and Peter remembered the Lord's words when he had said to him, 'Before the cock crows today, you will deny me three times.' And he went outside and wept bitterly. Meanwhile the men who were holding Jesus were mocking and beating him. They blindfolded him and questioned him, saying, 'Prophesy! Who hit you?' And they kept heaping many other insults on him.

When day broke a meeting of the elders of the people, the chief priests and scribes was convened, and they brought him before their council, saying, 'If you are the Messiah, tell us.' But he said to them, 'If I tell you, you will not believe, and if I question you, you will not answer. But from now on, the *Son of man* will be *seated at the right hand* of the Power *of God*. They all said, 'So you are the Son of God?' He answered, 'You say that I am.' Then they said, 'Why do we still need any evidence? We have heard it ourselves from his own lips.'

The whole gathering then rose and brought him before Pilate.

They began to accuse him, saying, 'We found this man inciting our people to revolt, forbidding payment of taxes to Caesar, and claiming to be the Messiah, a king.' Pilate asked him, 'Are you the king of the Jews?' He replied, 'You say so.' Pilate then said to the chief priests and the crowds, 'I find no case against this man.' But they insisted, 'He is stirring up the people, teaching all over Judaea and starting from Galilee all the way to this place.' Hearing this, Pilate asked if the man were a Galilean; and having discovered that he came under Herod's jurisdiction, he sent him off to Herod, who was also in Jerusalem at that time.

Herod was delighted to see Jesus; he had been wanting for a long time to set eyes on him; moreover, he was hoping to see some sign done by him. So he questioned him at some length, but without getting any reply. Meanwhile the chief priests and the scribes were there, vehemently pressing their accusations. Then Herod, together with his guards, treated him with contempt and made fun of him; he put a rich cloak on him and sent him back to Pilate. And Herod and Pilate became friends that day, though formerly they had been at enmity with each other.

Pilate then summoned the chief priests and the leading men and the people, and said to them, 'You brought this man before me as inciting the people to revolt. See, I have examined him in your presence and found no case against this man in any of the charges you bring against him. Neither has Herod, since he has sent him back to us. See, he has done nothing that deserves death, so I shall have him beaten and release him.' But as one man they all howled, 'Take this man away! Release Barabbas for us!' (This man had been thrown into prison because of a riot in the city and murder.)

Again Pilate addressed them, wanting to release Jesus again, but they swelled their shouting, 'Crucify! Crucify him!' And for a third time he spoke to them, 'But what evil has this man done? I have found no case against him that deserves death, so I shall have him beaten and release him.' But they insisted, demanding at the top of their voices, that he should be crucified. And their voices prevailed.

Pilate then gave his verdict, that their demand was to be granted. He released the man they asked for, who had been imprisoned for riot and murder, and handed Jesus over to them as they wished.

HOLY WEEK

As they were leading him away they seized on a man, Simon from Cyrene, who was coming from the country, and laid on him the cross to carry behind Jesus. A large number of the people followed him, and women, who beat their breasts and mourned for him. But Jesus turned to them and said, 'Daughters of Jerusalem, do not weep for me; but weep for yourselves and for your children. For look, the days are coming when people will say, "Blessed are the barren, the wombs that have not borne children, the breasts that have not given suck!" Then they will begin to *say to the mountains, "Fall on us!" and to the hills, "Cover us!"* For if they do this when the wood is green, what will they do when it is dry?' Two others also, criminals, were led out to be put to death with him.

When they reached the place called The Skull, there they crucified him and the criminals, one on his right, the other on his left. Jesus said, 'Father, forgive them; for they do not know what they are doing.' Then they cast lots to share out his clothing. The people stood watching. As for the leaders, they scoffed at him saying, 'He saved others, let him save himself if he is the Messiah of God, the Chosen One.' The soldiers mocked him too, coming up to him, offering him vinegar, and saying, 'If you are the king of the Jews, save yourself.' There was also an inscription over him: 'This is the King of the Jews'.

One of the criminals hanging there jeered at him: 'Are you not the Messiah? Save yourself and us.' But in reply the other rebuked him saying. 'Do you not fear God, since you are under the same sentence? And we justly, for we are getting what we deserve for what we did. But this man did nothing wrong.' Then he said, 'Jesus, remember me when you come into your kingdom.' He answered him, 'Amen I say to you, today you will be with me in paradise.'

It was now about noon and darkness came over the whole land until mid-afternoon, as the sun's light failed. The curtain of the Temple was torn right down the middle. Jesus cried out in a loud voice saying, 'Father, *into your hands I commit my spirit.*' Having said this, he breathed his last. When the centurion saw what had taken place, he gave glory to God and said, 'Truly, this was a just man.' And when all the crowds who had gathered for the spectacle saw what had happened, they went home beating their breasts. All his friends stood at a distance, and also the women who had followed with him from Galilee, watching these things.

Now a man named Joseph, a member of the council, a good and righteous man, had not agreed with their plan and their action. He came from Arimathaea, a Jewish town, and was awaiting the kingdom of God. This man approached Pilate and asked for the body of Jesus. Then he took it down, wrapped it in a linen cloth and laid it in a rock-hewn tomb in which no one had ever yet been laid. It was the day of preparation and the Sabbath was beginning to grow light. The women who had come from Galilee with Jesus followed behind and saw the tomb and how the body had been laid. They went back and prepared spices and ointments. And on the Sabbath day they rested, in accordance with the commandment.

THE STORY OF THE Passion in Luke begins with an extended account of the last supper, which preserves several unique sayings of Jesus, among them the words of Jesus to Simon Peter that he should strengthen his brothers. On the Mount of Olives Jesus is comforted while at prayer by an 'angel from heaven'. Luke describes the disciples as sleeping 'from grief'. He avoids the painful kiss of Judas and reports the healing of the ear of the high priest's servant. Luke also reduces the vehemence of the denials of Peter and finishes that scene with the Lord turning and 'looking straight at Peter', as Peter breaks down and weeps. The interrogation begins at dawn and the scene then transfers to Pilate's palace. Pilate asserts three times that he finds no guilt in Jesus, which seems to be Luke's way of showing that the Roman power should not oppose the Christian preaching. Herod Antipas is 'delighted' to see Jesus and cynically clothes him with 'a rich cloak', but Luke reports no scourging or crowning with thorns. On the way to Calvary the women weep for Jesus, while Jesus speaks words of forgiveness to his executioners, pardons the thief who turns to him, and ends his life with words from Psalm 31: 'Into your hands I commit my spirit'. The aftermath of the crucifixion shows the crowds returning home 'beating their breasts'.

Why does Luke play down the violence of the Passion story?
We pray for the gift of forgiveness for ourselves, and as a gift to be offered to others.

HOLY WEEK

MONDAY IN HOLY WEEK

A reading from the prophet Isaiah (42:1-7)
Here is my servant whom I uphold,
my chosen one in whom my soul delights.
I have put my spirit upon him,
he will bring fair judgement to the nations.
He will not cry out or raise his voice,
his voice will not be heard in the street.
A crushed reed he will not break
nor will he snuff out a faltering wick.
He will establish fair judgement for the nations.
He will not grow faint or be discouraged
until he has established fair judgement on earth
and the coastlands are waiting for his guidance.
Thus says God, the Lord,
who created the heavens and spread them out,
who hammered into shape the earth and what comes from it,
who gave breath to the people upon it
and spirit to those who walk on it:
'I the Lord have called you in righteousness,
I have grasped you by the hand and watched over you;
I have given you as a covenant for the people
and light for the nations,
to open the eyes of the blind,
to free captives from prison,
and those who sit in darkness from the dungeon.

THE SONGS OF THE suffering Servant are read on Monday, Tuesday, Wednesday and Friday of Holy Week. This first song describes the Servant as the 'chosen one', chosen by God, who bestows the spirit on him. Three times it is stated that he is to bring 'fair judgement' (*mishpat*). His style is humble and respectful, not cruel and domineering. He does not break a 'crushed reed', nor extinguish a 'faltering wick'. He will persevere because God has given him strength, for even the 'coastlands' await his guidance. The creator God then gives a solemn declaration: God has called this servant 'in righteousness' (*tsedeq*) and protected him. He has given him 'as a covenant', so that peoples will live in peace, and there will be harmony between nations. The light which the Servant brings must extend to the nations (*goyim*). He will 'open the eyes of the blind' and 'free captives from prison'. Isaiah 61, read at the Mass of Chrism, will see a similar mission given to the one who says 'the spirit of the Lord is upon me'. The poem prepares for the humility and universal mission of Christ to bring freedom, justice and peace.

> **Psalm 27 (26)** This psalm proclaims that the Lord brings light and salvation.

A reading from the holy gospel according to John (12:1-11)

Six days before the Passover, Jesus went to Bethany, where Lazarus was, whom he had raised from the dead. They gave a dinner for him there; Martha waited on them and Lazarus was one of those at table. Mary brought in a pound of very costly ointment, pure nard, and anointed the feet of Jesus, wiping them with her hair; the house was filled with the scent of the ointment. Then Judas Iscariot – one of his disciples, the man who was to betray him – said, 'Why was this ointment not sold for three hundred denarii and the money given to the poor?' He said this, not because he cared about the poor, but because he was a thief; he was in charge of the common fund and used to steal from the contents. So Jesus said, 'Leave her alone, so that she may keep it for the day of my burial. You have the poor with you always, you will not always have me.'

A great crowd of Jews heard that he was there and came not only on account of Jesus but also to see Lazarus whom he had raised from the dead. Then the chief priests planned to kill Lazarus as well, since it was on his account that many of the Jews were leaving them and believing in Jesus.

ONLY THE FOURTH GOSPEL reports an anointing of the feet of Jesus by Mary, sister of Martha and Lazarus, at their house in Bethany, on the day before he enters Jerusalem. Mark 14 and Matthew 26 recount an anointing of the head of Jesus at the house of Simon some days after his entry to the holy city. This event happens six days before the Passover and so is appropriately read on this day. Unlike Matthew's story of the anointing, at which the disciples complain about the waste, here it is Judas who complains about the cost of the ointment. This adds to the negative portrayal of Judas, who is then described as a 'thief'. The action of Mary, by contrast, will be remembered as an act of love. A 'great crowd' gathers, to see Jesus, but also to see Lazarus, whom Jesus raised from the dead. Ironically and tragically the chief priests plot to kill Lazarus too.

While Jesus offers life, his opponents are intent on bringing death. Pray for a spirit of life-giving generosity.

TUESDAY IN HOLY WEEK

A reading from the prophet Isaiah (49:1-6)

Listen to me, coastlands,
pay attention, far distant peoples!
The LORD called me from the womb,
before my birth he pronounced my name.
He made my mouth like a sharp sword,
he hid me in the shadow of his hand.
He made me into a sharpened arrow
and concealed me in his quiver.
He said to me, 'Israel, you are my servant,
through whom I manifest my glory.'
But I said, 'In vain have I toiled;
for nothing, to no purpose have I spent my strength.'
Yet all the while my cause is with the LORD
and my reward with my God.
And now the LORD has spoken,
who formed me from the womb to be his servant,
to bring Jacob back to him and for Israel to be gathered to him.
I shall be honoured in the LORD's eyes,
and my God has been my strength.
He said, 'It is too light a task that you should be my servant,
to restore the tribes of Jacob and bring back the survivors of Israel;

I shall make you a light to the nations
so that my salvation may reach to the ends of the earth.'

THE SERVANT SAYS HE was called to speak 'from the womb' like Jeremiah (Jeremiah 1). He uses the images of 'sword' and 'arrow', for he is called to address those who are near and the distant 'coastlands' too. The Servant is addressed as 'Israel' but the mission is also to Israel, so that the true identity of the Servant is unsure. He loses hope and says 'in vain have I toiled', and his words recall those in the 'confessions' of Jeremiah (Jeremiah 15 and 20). Yet he is still confident that his 'cause' (*mishpat*) is with the Lord. The Lord gives him reassurance, for his task is not only to 'bring back the survivors of Israel' from exile, and to reunite the people, but also to bring 'a light to the nations' (*goyim*), and salvation reaching to 'the ends of the earth'. This universal mission, not without trials, is reflected in that of Christ and of the Church.

> **Psalm 71 (70)** God is described as 'rock', 'refuge' and 'stronghold'.

A reading from the holy gospel according to John (13:21-33, 36-38)

Having said this, Jesus was deeply disturbed and bore witness, 'Amen, Amen I say to you, one of you will betray me.' The disciples looked at one another, wondering whom he meant. One of his disciples, the one whom Jesus loved, was reclining next to Jesus, so Simon Peter signed to him to ask whom he meant. Leaning back just at Jesus' chest he said to him, 'Lord, who is it?' Jesus answered, 'It is the one for whom I dip the piece of bread and give to him.' Then dipping the piece of bread he gave it to Judas, son of Simon Iscariot. And after the piece of bread then Satan entered into him. Jesus then said, 'What you are doing, do quickly.' None of the others at table understood why he said this to him. Some thought, since Judas held the common fund, that Jesus was telling him, 'Buy what we need for the festival,' or to give something to the poor. Taking the piece of bread, he immediately went out. It was night.

When he had gone out, Jesus said:
'Now has the Son of man been glorified,

and God has been glorified in him.
If God has been glorified in him,
God will glorify him in himself,
and will glorify him at once.
Little children,
yet a little while I am with you.
You will look for me,
and, as I told the Jews,
and I now say to you,
where I am going
you cannot come.

Simon Peter said, 'Lord, where are you going?' Jesus replied, 'Where I am going you cannot follow me now, but you shall follow later.' Peter said to him, 'Lord, why cannot I follow you now? I will lay down my life for you.' Jesus answered, 'Will you lay down your life for me? Amen, Amen I say to you, before the cock crows you will have disowned me three times.'

THE CONTEXT IS THE supper on the night of Jesus' arrest. Jesus is distressed as he considers the forthcoming betrayal by Judas. Judas features in the gospel every day as the Easter Triduum approaches, but his presence is particularly threatening in this passage from John. It is 'the disciple whom Jesus loved' who asks the identity of the traitor. Jesus then offers a piece of bread to Judas. We can recall the words of Psalm 41, 'even my friend, in whom I trusted, who ate my bread, makes coarse gestures against me'. The traitor is identified in the violation of table fellowship. The evangelist continues, 'Satan entered into him', and Jesus himself commands him to leave. As Judas goes out from the supper darkest night descends. Jesus now begins a long discourse that, with some interjections from the disciples, will conclude only in John 17. He speaks of his being 'glorified', for it is in his death that God is glorified. Peter vows to give his life for Jesus, but Jesus knows that he will fall short. Jesus foresees his weakness and his denials, which are reported without elaboration in chapter 18, and will be read on Good Friday.

How is betrayal possible by those who are closest to Jesus?
Pray for the gift of fidelity despite disappointment.

WEDNESDAY IN HOLY WEEK

A reading from the prophet Isaiah (50:4-9)

The Lord GOD has given me a disciple's tongue,
to know how to comfort the weary with a word.
Morning by morning he sharpens my ear
to listen like a disciple.
The Lord GOD has opened my ear
and I did not rebel or turn away.
I offered my back to those who struck me,
my cheeks to those who plucked my beard;
I did not turn away my face from insult and spitting.
The Lord GOD comes to my help:
therefore no insult has touched me,
therefore I have set my face like flint.
I know that I shall not be shamed.
He who grants me saving justice is near!
Who will bring a case against me?
Let us appear in court together!
Who has a case against me?
Let him approach me!
Look, the Lord GOD is coming to my help!
Who will condemn me?

THE SPEAKER IN THIS third song is called to 'comfort the weary', day by day learning new things in discipleship. His prophetic vocation has much in common with the situation of the prophet Jeremiah. Despite his commitment to the good of the people, he suffers punishment and abuse, even 'insult and spitting'. The Lord is with him nevertheless. He sets his face 'like flint', just as Jeremiah was told that 'I have made you a pillar of iron, a wall of bronze' (Jeremiah 1:18). When threatened with a case against him he is confident of the Lord's vindication. It is easy to see how the details of this particular poem led it to be considered a preparation for the sufferings of Christ.

> **Psalm 69 (68)** The psalm matches the situation of the reading, and expresses similar trust.

A reading from the holy gospel according to Matthew (26:14-25)

Then one of the Twelve, the man called Judas Iscariot, went to the chief priests and said, 'What are you prepared to give me if I hand him over to you?' They settled with him for thirty silver pieces, and from then onwards he began to look for an opportunity to betray him.

Now on the first day of Unleavened Bread the disciples came to Jesus to say, 'Where do you want us to make the preparations for you to eat the Passover?' He said, 'Go to a certain man in the city and say to him, "The teacher says: My time is near. It is at your house that I am keeping Passover with my disciples."' The disciples did what Jesus told them and prepared the Passover. When evening came he was at table with the Twelve. And while they were eating he said, 'Amen I say to you, one of you is about to betray me.' They were greatly distressed and started asking him in turn, 'Not me, Lord, surely?' He answered, 'Someone who has dipped his hand into the dish with me will betray me. The Son of man is going to his fate, as it is written about him, but alas for that man by whom the Son of man is betrayed! It would have been better for that man if he had never been born!' Judas, who was to betray him, asked in his turn, 'Not me, Rabbi, surely?' Jesus answered, 'It is you who said it.'

THESE ARE THE OPENING verses of the story of the Passion in the gospel of Matthew. Judas Iscariot, one of the twelve, takes the initiative and volunteers his assistance to the chief priests in return for the meagre sum of thirty silver pieces. Jesus instructs the disciples to prepare for the Passover feast, referring to himself as 'the teacher' (*didaskalos*) (Matthew 23:8) and declaring that the 'time' (*kairos*) has come. The first words of Jesus at the feast focus on the betrayal and its instigator. While the other disciples address Jesus as 'Lord', Judas says 'Not me, Rabbi, surely?' His tone is markedly different from theirs. The gospel passage ends with Judas, as it had begun, but Jesus goes to the cross not because Judas has betrayed him but out of love and commitment to the truth.

READING THE BIBLE THROUGH LENT

How should we prepare for difficult times in our lives?
Pray for those who are fearful of the future.

HOLY THURSDAY
MASS OF CHRISM

A reading from the prophet Isaiah (61:1-3, 6, 8-9)
The spirit of Lord God is on me
for the Lord has anointed me.
He has sent me to bring good news to the afflicted,
to soothe the broken-hearted,
to proclaim liberty to captives,
release to those in prison,
to proclaim a year of the Lord's favour,
a day of vindication for our God,
to comfort those who mourn,
to give to those who mourn for Zion
a headdress in place of ashes,
a garland in place of mourning-dress,
the oil of gladness in place of a drooping spirit.
But you shall be called 'priests of the Lord'
and addressed as ministers of our God.
 I shall reward them faithfully
and make an everlasting covenant with them.
Their race will be known among the nations
and their descendants amid the peoples.
All who see them will agree
that they are a people blessed by the Lord.

THE MASS OF CHRISM, celebrated on the morning of Holy Thursday, takes its name from the oil of chrism, used at Baptism, Confirmation and Ordination. At this Mass all the holy oils are blessed. The prophetic figure in this reading, anointed by the Spirit to 'bring good news', prepares the way for the Christ, the Messiah, whose name means 'anointed one'. To be anointed to 'bring the good news' is common to all Christians. The 'oil of gladness' is given above all to those whose hearts are broken, whose spirit is 'drooping'. The people are called to be 'priests of the Lord' and God declares, 'I shall reward them faithfully and make an everlasting covenant with them.' They are a people 'blessed by the Lord'.

> **Psalm 89 (88)** God has 'found' David and anointed him with holy oil.

A reading from the book of the Apocalypse (1:5-8)

Grace and peace to you from Jesus Christ, the faithful witness, the first-born from the dead, the ruler of the kings of the earth. To him who loves us and has freed us from our sins by his blood, and made us a kingdom, priests to his God and Father; to him be glory and power for ever and ever. Amen. Look, he is coming on the clouds; every eye shall see him, even those who pierced him, and all the races of the earth will mourn over him. So it shall be. Amen. 'I am the Alpha and the Omega,' says the Lord God, who is, who was, and who is to come, the Almighty.

THE OPENING WORDS OF the book of the Apocalypse speak of Jesus Christ as 'witness' (*martus*). He it is who loves us and has freed us from sin. By his death he makes us 'a kingdom, priests to his God and Father'. At his coming 'every eye' shall see him, and all races will mourn over him. The majestic words of God 'I am the Alpha and the Omega' will be repeated towards the end of the book. God's use of the first and last letters of the Greek alphabet indicates dominion over everything, and God brings together the three dimensions of time: 'I am the One who is, who was, and who is to come.'

A reading from the holy gospel according to Luke (4:16-21)

Jesus came to Nazara, where he had been brought up, and went into the synagogue on the Sabbath as was his custom. He stood up to read, and he was given the scroll of the prophet Isaiah. Unrolling the scroll he found the place where it is written:

*The spirit of the Lord is upon me,
for he has anointed me to bring good news to the poor.
He has sent me to proclaim release to captives,
sight to the blind, to let the oppressed go free,
to proclaim a year of the Lord's favour.*

He then rolled up the scroll, gave it back to the assistant and sat down. And the eyes of all in the synagogue were fixed on him. Then he began to speak to them, 'Today this text has been fulfilled in your hearing.'

CHRIST, WHO HAS DIED, is risen, and will come again, is the one who is 'anointed' with the Spirit to bring good news. He is anointed by Mary for burial (John 12). His status is challenged by the high priest: 'Are you the Christ?' (Mark 14) And by Pontius Pilate: 'Are you the king of the Jews?' (Mark 15) He is the Christ, but 'the crucified Christ', whom St Paul will call 'the power of God and the wisdom of God' (1 Corinthians 1). He is the fulfilment of Scripture who anoints his followers in Baptism to bring good news to the poor.

As a follower of the crucified Christ, am I worthy to be called 'Christian'?
Pray for the grace to embrace the paschal mystery of Christ.

HOLY THURSDAY
MASS OF THE LORD'S SUPPER

A reading from the book of Exodus (12:1-8, 11-14)

The LORD said to Moses and Aaron in Egypt, 'This month must be the first of all the months for you, the first month of your year. Speak to the whole community of Israel saying, "On the tenth day of this month each man must take an animal from the flock for his family: one animal for each household. If the household is too small for the animal, he must join with his neighbour nearest to his house, depending on the number of persons. When you choose the animal, you will take into account what each can eat. It must be an animal without blemish, a male, one year old; you shall take it either from the sheep or from the goats. You must keep it till the fourteenth day of the month when the whole assembly of the community of Israel will slaughter it at twilight. They shall take some of the blood and put it on both doorposts and the lintel of the houses where it is eaten. That night, they shall eat meat, roasted over the fire, with unleavened bread and bitter herbs. This is how you must eat it: with a belt around your waist, your sandals on your feet and your staff in your hand. You must eat it hurriedly: it is a Passover for the Lord. That night, I shall go through the land of Egypt and strike down all the first-born in the land of Egypt, human and animal alike, and I shall execute justice on all the gods of Egypt. I am the Lord! The blood will be a sign for you on the houses where you are. When I see the blood I shall pass over you, and you will escape the destructive plague when I strike the land of Egypt. This day must be commemorated by you, and you must keep it as a festival for the Lord. You must keep it as a feast-day for all generations; this is a decree for all time."'

THE SUFFERING AND DEATH of Jesus takes place at the time of the Jewish feast of Passover. This first reading of the Mass of the Lord's Supper on the evening of Holy Thursday gives us the instructions for celebrating the feast. Jesus not only celebrated Passover with the disciples on the night before he died, but in celebrating it he transformed the rite. While Passover for Jews, together with the observance of Unleavened Bread, recalls the liberation from Egypt, and a new life of freedom, the Christian Eucharist celebrates freedom from sin and death through the self-giving of the Son of God. Blood figures in both rites. The blood of the lamb sprinkled on doorposts and lintel is a sign of freedom. The blood of Christ, the new Lamb, consumed by Christians, is a memorial of the death of Jesus for all those who believe in him, as they share in his life-giving death.

> **Psalm 116 (115)** 'The cup of salvation' is raised. The 'death of his faithful' is precious to God.

READING THE BIBLE THROUGH LENT

A reading from the first letter of St Paul to the Corinthians (11:23-26)

For the tradition I received from the Lord and also handed on to you is that on the night he was betrayed, the Lord Jesus took some bread, and after he had given thanks, he broke it, and he said, 'This is my body, which is for you; do this in remembrance of me.' And in the same way with the cup after supper, saying, 'This cup is the new covenant in my blood. Whenever you drink it, do this in remembrance of me.' As often as you eat this bread, then, and drink this cup, you are proclaiming the Lord's death until he comes.

THE ACCOUNT OF THE Last Supper by St Paul given here is probably the oldest account we have, and is reflected in those of Matthew, Mark and especially Luke. Jesus speaks of his very presence in the bread and wine which is shared. For each of the actions the disciples are told to 'do this in remembrance of me'. This 'memorial', like the Passover before it, is a full and real making present of the gift of salvation. Paul adds his own words, that the eating and drinking are a 'proclamation' of the Lord's death 'until he comes'. Taking part in this memorial of the new covenant is our sharing with Christ in his death and resurrection, with all who eat this bread, and with all for whom he died.

A reading from the holy gospel according to John (13:1-15)

Before the festival of the Passover, Jesus, knowing that his hour had come to pass from this world to the Father, having loved those who were his in the world, loved them to the end.

They were at supper, and the devil had already put it into the heart of Judas Iscariot son of Simon, to betray him. Jesus, knowing that the Father had put everything into his hands, and that he had come from God and was returning to God, got up from the table, removed his outer garments and, taking a towel, wrapped it round his waist; he then poured water into a basin and began to wash the disciples' feet and to wipe them with the towel wrapped round his waist. He came to Simon Peter, who said to him, 'Lord, are you going to wash my feet?' Jesus answered, 'At the moment you do not know what I am doing, but later you will understand.' Peter said, 'You shall never wash my feet.' Jesus replied, 'If I do not wash you, you have no share with me.' Simon Peter said, 'Lord, not only my feet, but my hands and my head as well!' Jesus said to him, 'No one who has had a bath needs washing except for the feet. Such a person is entirely clean. You too are clean, though not all of you.' He knew who was to betray him. That was why he said, 'though not all of you'.

When he had washed their feet he put on his outer garments and reclined again at the table. He said to them, 'Do you know what I have done to you? You call me Teacher and Lord, and rightly, for so I am. If I, then, the Teacher and Lord, have washed your feet, you also ought to wash one another's feet. I have given you an example so that as I have done to you, you also should do.'

THE FOURTH GOSPEL OFFERS us this account which in its own way reflects the meaning and poignancy of the night before Jesus died. The presence of Judas is indicated in the opening words, for Judas will only leave the gathering later (John 13:30). There is extraordinary detail and deliberation in the description of the actions of Jesus. Peter makes his principled objection, only to proceed to the opposite extreme once Jesus explains what he is doing. A further allusion to betrayal comes in Jesus' assertion that not all of them are 'clean'. The command to do as Jesus has done is followed by the 'new commandment' to love one another in imitation of Jesus (John 13:34). The proximity of the Passion and death suggests that love 'to the end' is particularly demanding.

How should we follow the example of Jesus?
Pray for all for whom religion is empty words and gestures, with no heart.

GOOD FRIDAY

A reading from the prophet Isaiah (52:13-53:12)
Look, my servant will prosper;
he will be lifted up, will rise to great heights.
Just as many people were appalled at him –
he was so inhumanly disfigured

that he no longer looked like a man –
so will he astonish many nations.
Kings will keep silence before him,
for they shall see what had never been told,
understand what they had never heard.
Who would believe what we have heard?
To whom has the Lord's power been revealed?
He grew up before the Lord like a sapling,
like a root in arid ground.
He had no beauty, no majesty to attract us,
no appearance to win our hearts;
he was despised, shunned by the people,
a man of sorrows, familiar with suffering,
one from whom people avert their gaze,
despised, and we held him of no account.
Yet ours were the sufferings he bore,
ours the sorrows he carried.
We thought of him as smitten,
struck down by God and afflicted;
yet he was wounded for our rebellions,
crushed on account of our evil deeds.
The punishment that made us whole was on him:
his wounds brought healing to us.
We had all gone astray like sheep,
each taking our own way,
and the Lord laid upon him
the iniquity of us all.
Afflicted and humbled, he never opened his mouth;
like a lamb led to the slaughterhouse,
like a sheep dumb before its shearers,
he never opened his mouth.
Forcibly, without justice, he was taken
and who gives a thought to his fate?
He was cut off from the land of the living,
the sin of his people visited upon him.
He was given a grave with the wicked
and his tomb is with the rich,

although he had done no violence,
no deceit upon his lips.
It was the Lord's good pleasure to crush him.
If he gives his life as a sin offering,
he will see his descendants and live long.
Through him the Lord's good pleasure will succeed.
After his anguish, he will see the light and be content.
By his knowledge my servant,
the righteous one, will justify many
by taking their guilt on himself.
Hence I shall give him a portion with the great
and he will share the spoil with the mighty
for having exposed himself to death
and for being counted among the rebellious.
Yet he was bearing the sin of many
and interceding for the rebellious.

THIS MAJESTIC POEM ABOUT death and resurrection is the fourth and last song of the suffering servant. It combines words of God, addressing 'my servant' at the beginning and the end of the song, with words of the people and words of the prophet. While the third song had begun to speak of the abuse of the servant, this song adds to the experience of suffering the question of meaning, for the servant, who was 'wounded for our rebellions', is said to 'justify many' and to 'take their guilt' on himself. This should be understood as a particularly profound reflection on the meaning of innocent suffering. The poem ends with the prospect of triumph. The fourth song of the suffering servant is the first text which comes to mind when the words of Paul are recalled, that Christ Jesus died 'according to the Scriptures' (1 Corinthians 15:3), words also taken up in the Nicene Creed.

> **Psalm 31 (30)** The psalmist says: 'Into your hands I commit my spirit'. Despite becoming an 'object of scorn' he is confident of salvation.

A reading from the letter to the Hebrews (4:14-16, 5:7-9)

Since in Jesus, the Son of God, we have the supreme high priest who has gone through to the highest heaven, let us hold firm to our profession of faith. For the high priest we have is not incapable of feeling our weaknesses with us, but has been put to the test in exactly the same way as ourselves, apart from sin. Let us, then, approach the throne of grace with confidence to receive mercy and to find grace in time of need.

During the days of his flesh, he offered up prayer and entreaty, with loud cries and with tears, to the one who had the power to save him from death, and, winning a hearing by his reverence, he learnt obedience, Son though he was, through his sufferings; when he had been perfected, he became for all who obey him the source of eternal salvation.

THE LETTER TO THE Hebrews describes Christ as the high priest of the new covenant, one who is trustworthy and merciful. He has been put to the test just as we are. He is like us in all things but sin. The final verses of this reading recall his prayer in Gethsemane, where he 'learnt obedience'. Coming to 'perfection' he offers salvation to all who obey him.

The passion of our Lord Jesus Christ according to John (18:1 – 19:42)

After he had said this, Jesus went out with his disciples across the Kidron valley where there was a garden, which he and his disciples entered. Judas the traitor also knew the place, since Jesus had often met his disciples there, so Judas brought the cohort to this place together with officers from the chief priests and the Pharisees, all with lanterns and torches and weapons. Knowing everything that was to happen to him, Jesus came forward and said, 'Who are you looking for?' They answered him, 'Jesus the Nazarene.' He said, 'I am he.' Now Judas the traitor was standing among them. When Jesus said to them, 'I am he,' they moved back and fell to the ground. Again he asked them, 'Who are you looking for?' They said, 'Jesus the Nazarene.' Jesus replied, 'I told you that I am he. If you are looking for me, let these others go.' This was to fulfil the words he had spoken, 'Not one of those you gave me have I lost.'

HOLY WEEK

Simon Peter, who had a sword, drew it, struck the high priest's servant, and cut off his right ear. The servant's name was Malchus. Jesus said to Peter, 'Put your sword back in its scabbard; am I not to drink the cup that the Father has given me?'

The cohort and its tribune and the officers of the Jews seized Jesus and bound him. They took him first to Annas, because Annas was the father-in-law of Caiaphas, who was high priest that year. It was Caiaphas who had advised the Jews that it was better for one man to die for the people.

Simon Peter, with another disciple, followed Jesus. This disciple, who was known to the high priest, went with Jesus into the high priest's palace, but Peter stayed outside at the door. So the other disciple, the one known to the high priest, went out, spoke to the door-keeper and brought Peter in. The girl on duty at the door said to Peter, 'Are you not also one of that man's disciples?' He answered, 'I am not.' Now it was cold, and the servants and officers had made a charcoal fire and were standing there warming themselves. Peter stood there too, warming himself with them.

The high priest questioned Jesus about his disciples and his teaching. Jesus answered, 'I have spoken openly to the world; I have always taught in the synagogue and in the Temple where all the Jews meet together; I have said nothing in secret. Why ask me? Ask those who heard what I taught; they know what I said.' At these words, one of the officers standing by gave Jesus a slap in the face, saying, 'Is that how you answer the high priest?' Jesus replied, 'If I have spoken wrongly, attest the wrong; but if I have spoken rightly, why do you strike me?' Then Annas sent him, bound, to Caiaphas the high priest.

Simon Peter stood there warming himself, and they said to him, 'Are you not also one of his disciples?' He denied it saying, 'I am not.' One of the high priest's servants, a relation of the man whose ear Peter had cut off, said, 'Did I not see you in the garden with him?' Again Peter denied it, and at once a cock crowed.

They then led Jesus from the house of Caiaphas to the Praetorium. It was early morning. They did not go into the Praetorium themselves to avoid becoming defiled and in order to be able to eat the Passover. So Pilate came out to them and said, 'What charge do you bring against this man?' They replied, 'If he were not a criminal, we would not have handed him over to you.' Pilate said, 'Take him yourselves, and try him by your own Law.' The Jews answered, 'We are not allowed to put anyone to death.' This was to fulfil the words Jesus had spoken indicating by what kind of death he was going to die. So Pilate went back into the Praetorium and called Jesus to him and asked him, 'Are you the king of the Jews?' Jesus replied, 'Do you ask this on your own account, or have others spoken to you about me?' Pilate answered, 'Am I a Jew? Your own people and the chief priests handed you over to me: what have you done?' Jesus replied, 'My kingdom is not of this world; if my kingdom were of this world, my officers would have fought to prevent me being surrendered to the Jews. As it is, my kingdom is not from here.' Pilate said, 'So, then you are a king?' Jesus answered, 'You say that I am a king. I was born for this, I came into the world for this, to bear witness to the truth; and everyone who belongs to the truth listens to my voice.' Pilate said to him, 'What is truth?' And so saying he went out again to the Jews and said, 'I find no case against him. But you have a custom that I release to you one prisoner at the Passover; would you like me, then, to release to you the king of the Jews?' At this they shouted back, 'Not this man, but Barabbas.' Barabbas was a bandit.

    Pilate then had Jesus taken away and scourged; and the soldiers, twisting thorns into a wreath, put it on his head and clothed him in a purple robe. They kept coming up to him and saying, 'Hail, king of the Jews!' and slapping him in the face.

    Pilate came outside again and said to them, 'Look, I am going to bring him out to you to let you know that I find no case against him.' Jesus then came out wearing the wreath of thorns and the purple robe. Pilate said, 'Here is the man.' When they saw him, the chief priests and the guards shouted, 'Crucify him! Crucify him!' Pilate said, 'Take him yourselves and crucify him: I find no case against him.' The Jews replied, 'We have a Law, and according to that Law he ought to die, because he has claimed to be Son of God.'

    When Pilate heard them say this he was more afraid. He entered the Praetorium again, and said to Jesus, 'Where are you from?' But Jesus gave him no answer. Pilate then said to him, 'Do you refuse to speak to me? Do you not know that I have authority to release you and authority to crucify you?' Jesus replied, 'You would have no authority

HOLY WEEK

over me at all if it had not been given you from above; that is why the man who handed me over to you has the greater guilt.'

From that moment Pilate sought to set him free, but the Jews cried out, 'If you set this man free you are no friend of Caesar's; everyone who makes himself king is defying Caesar.' Hearing these words, Pilate had Jesus brought out, and seated himself on the chair of judgement at a place called the Pavement, in Hebrew, Gabbatha. It was the day of preparation for the Passover, at about noon. Pilate said to the Jews, 'Here is your king.' But they shouted, 'Away with him, away with him, crucify him.' Pilate said, 'Shall I crucify your king?' The chief priests answered, 'We have no king but Caesar.' So at that Pilate handed him over to them to be crucified.

They then took Jesus, and carrying the cross for himself he went out to what is called the Place of the Skull, which is called in Hebrew, Golgotha, where they crucified him and with him two others, one on either side, Jesus being in the middle. Pilate wrote out a notice and fixed it to the cross; it read, 'Jesus the Nazarene, King of the Jews'. Many of the Jews read this notice because the place where Jesus was crucified was near the city, and the writing was in Hebrew, Latin and Greek. So the chief priests of the Jews said to Pilate, 'Do not write "King of the Jews", but "This man said, I am King of the Jews"'. Pilate answered, 'What I have written, I have written.'

When the soldiers had crucified Jesus they took his clothing and divided it into four shares, one for each soldier, and his tunic. His tunic was seamless, woven in one piece from the top right through; so they said to one another, 'Let us not tear it, but let us cast lots about it, whose it shall be.' This was to fulfil the words of scripture:

They divide my garments among them
and cast lots for my clothes.

That is what the soldiers did.

Near the cross of Jesus stood his mother and his mother's sister, Mary, the wife of Clopas, and Mary of Magdala. Seeing his mother and the disciple whom he loved standing near her, Jesus said to his mother, 'Woman, this is your son.' Then to the disciple he said, 'This is your mother.' And from that hour the disciple took her into his home.

After this, Jesus knowing that everything had now been completed and, so that the scripture should be fulfilled, he said:

'I am thirsty'

A jar full of sour wine stood there; so, putting a sponge soaked in the wine on a hyssop stick, they held it to his mouth. After Jesus had taken the wine he said, 'It is completed'; and bowing his head he gave over his spirit.

It was the day of preparation, and to avoid the bodies remaining on the cross during the Sabbath – since that Sabbath was a day of special dignity – the Jews asked Pilate to have their legs broken and the bodies taken away. Consequently the soldiers came and broke the legs of the first man and of the other who had been crucified with him. When they came to Jesus, they saw he was already dead, so they did not break his legs, but one of the soldiers pierced his side with a lance; and immediately there came out blood and water. The one who saw it has borne witness, and his witness is true, and he knows that he is telling the truth – so that you also may believe. For this happened that the scripture should be fulfilled,

None of his bones shall be broken;

and again, in another place scripture says,

They will look on the one they have pierced.

After this, Joseph of Arimathaea, who was a disciple of Jesus – though a secret one through fear of the Jews – asked Pilate to let him remove the body of Jesus. Pilate gave permission, so he came and took it away. Nicodemus came as well – the same one who had come to Jesus at night-time – and he brought a mixture of myrrh and aloes, weighing about fifty kilograms. They took the body of Jesus and wrapped it in linen cloths with the spices, according to the Jewish burial custom. In the place where he had been crucified there was a garden, and in this garden a new tomb in which no one had yet been laid. Since it was the day of preparation for the Jews and the tomb was nearby, they laid Jesus there.

THE ACCOUNT OF THE passion and death of Jesus in the Fourth Gospel offers a depth of reflection on these events. This is a considered meditation on the deepest reality of what happened to the Son of God. At the garden Jesus, 'knowing everything that was to happen to him', takes control, and those who come to arrest him prostrate themselves before him, as is appropriate before the light of God. Both Caiaphas, who had spoken earlier of the expediency of killing Jesus (John 11: 50), and his father-in-law Annas, are involved in interrogating Jesus. Pilate raises the issue of the kingship of Jesus, but Jesus has come 'to bear witness to the truth'. At Golgotha John has the poignant scene of the mother of Jesus, and the disciple Jesus loved. John repeatedly points to the fulfilment of Scripture, as when the garments of Jesus are shared out. The dying words of Jesus are in fact 'it is completed'. The piercing of the side of Jesus is another part of the narrative which is unique to the Fourth Gospel, and to which the evangelist solemnly testifies. Like the paschal lamb, 'none of his bones shall be broken'.

To what extent is John's story a revelation of the 'glory' of the Son of God?
May the different accounts of the Passion engage our minds and hearts.